Acetate Masters for Palm Tree Bible Stories Book 2

Illustrated by Arthur Baker

First published in 1998 in Great Britain by
KEVIN MAYHEW LTD
Rattlesden
Bury St Edmunds
Suffolk IP30 0SZ

ISBN 1 84003 146 8
Catalogue No 1396059

0 1 2 3 4 5 6 7 8 9

Illustrations by Arthur Baker
Cover designed by Jaquetta Sergeant
Printed in Great Britain

Contents

Noah's Big Boat

The full story is told in *Noah's Big Boat,*
ISBN 0 86209 359 7

Noah was a farmer and trusted God in all things.

But the rest of the people were very wicked and did not listen to God.

God spoke to Noah: 'Noah, I want you to build a very big boat.'

Then God said: 'Noah, load the boat with lots of food and round up the animals.' So Noah and his family got the animals in, two by two.

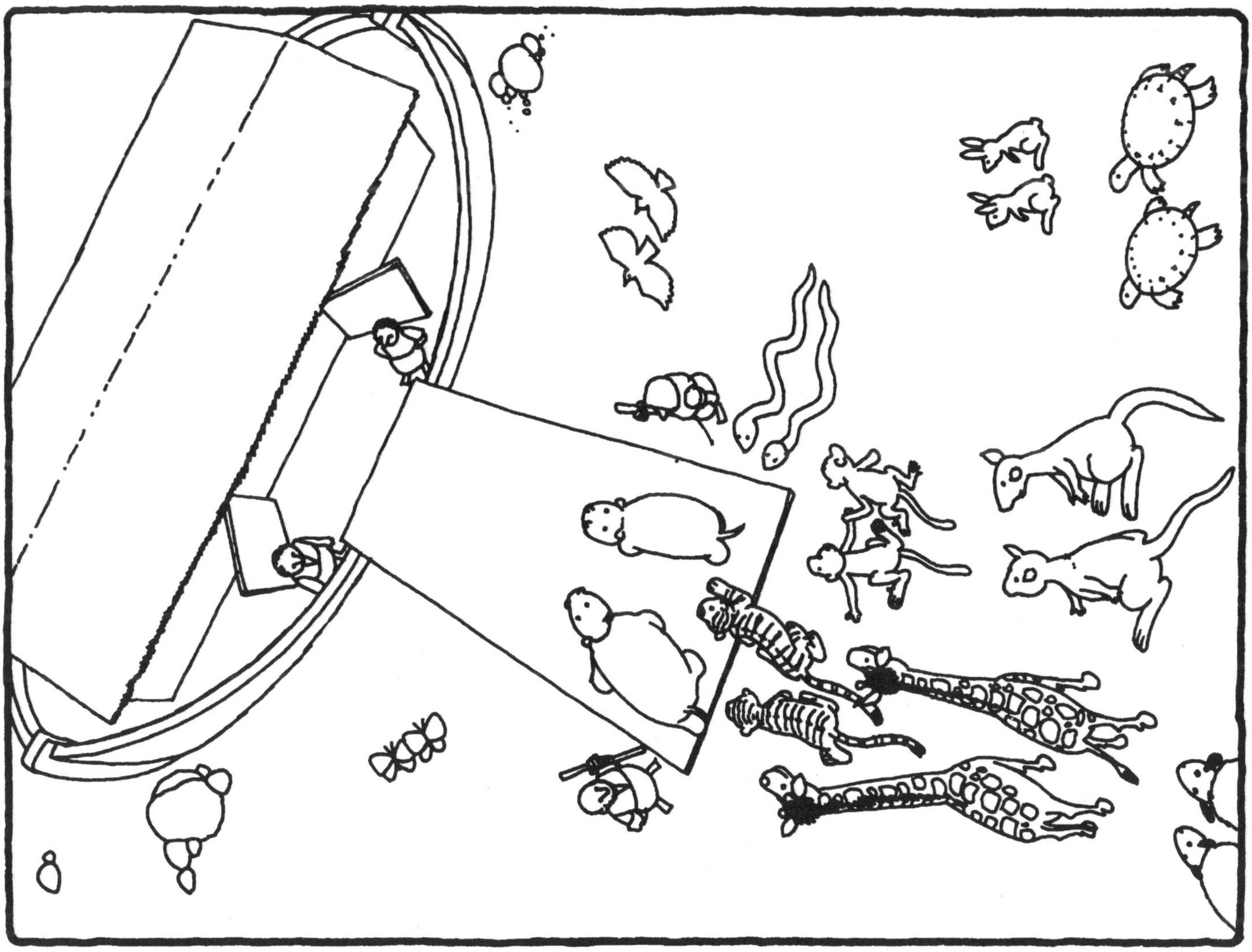

Then the first drops of rain fell. The rivers began to rise and burst their banks; the seas were raging storms; the towns were flooded. Soon, even the trees and mountains were covered by water.

At last the rain stopped. Noah sent out a dove and she came back with an olive leaf in her beak!

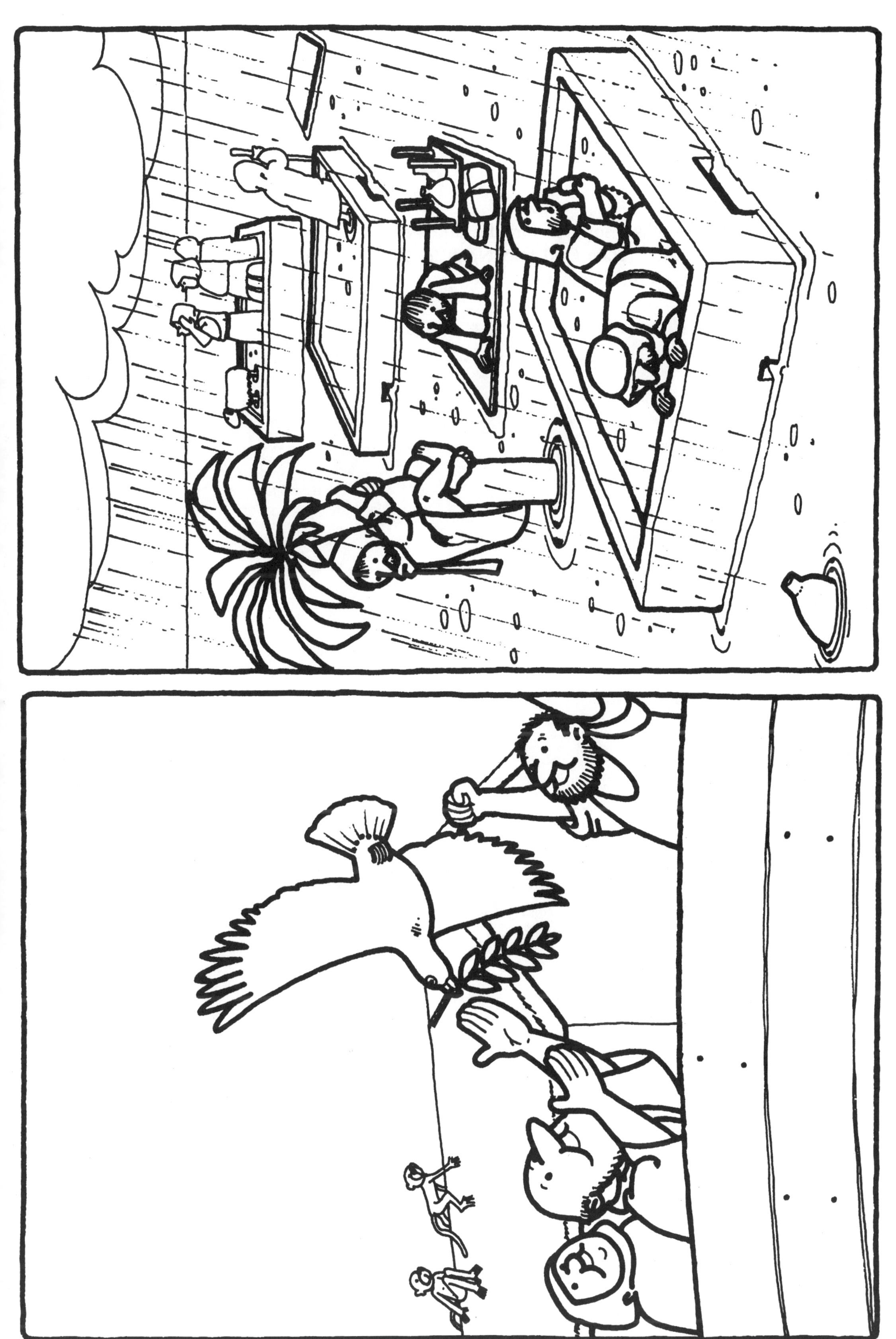

A few weeks went by before the land was dry enough to stand on. Then God told Noah to open the door and let out the animals.

God promised Noah and his family he would never again send such a big flood. He put a rainbow in the sky as a sign of his promise.

Baby in a Basket

The full story is told in *Baby in a Basket,*
ISBN 0 86209 425 9

Pharaoh had decided to kill all the Hebrews' new-born baby boys. A Hebrew family living near the palace were worried; Amran and his wife Jochebed were expecting another baby.

When the baby was born, it was a boy. Jochebed tried to hide the baby everywhere but eventually she could do so no longer. So, she made a beautiful basket for it and laid it among the bulrushes at the side of the river.

The princess was bathing in the river and found the basket. 'What a beautiful baby,' she said. 'He must belong to a Hebrew.'

Miriam, Jochebed's daughter came up to the princess and asked, 'Shall I find a Hebrew woman to nurse the baby?' 'Yes, please,' the princess replied. So Miriam fetched her mother who was asked by the princess to look after the baby, who she named Moses.

When Moses was older he went to live in the palace with the princess. But Moses knew he was a Hebrew. He knew that his own people were slaves to the Pharaoh.

'Just give Moses a few more years to grow into a fine strong man,' God thought to himself, 'then he will lead the Hebrews – my special people – to freedom in the Promised Land.'

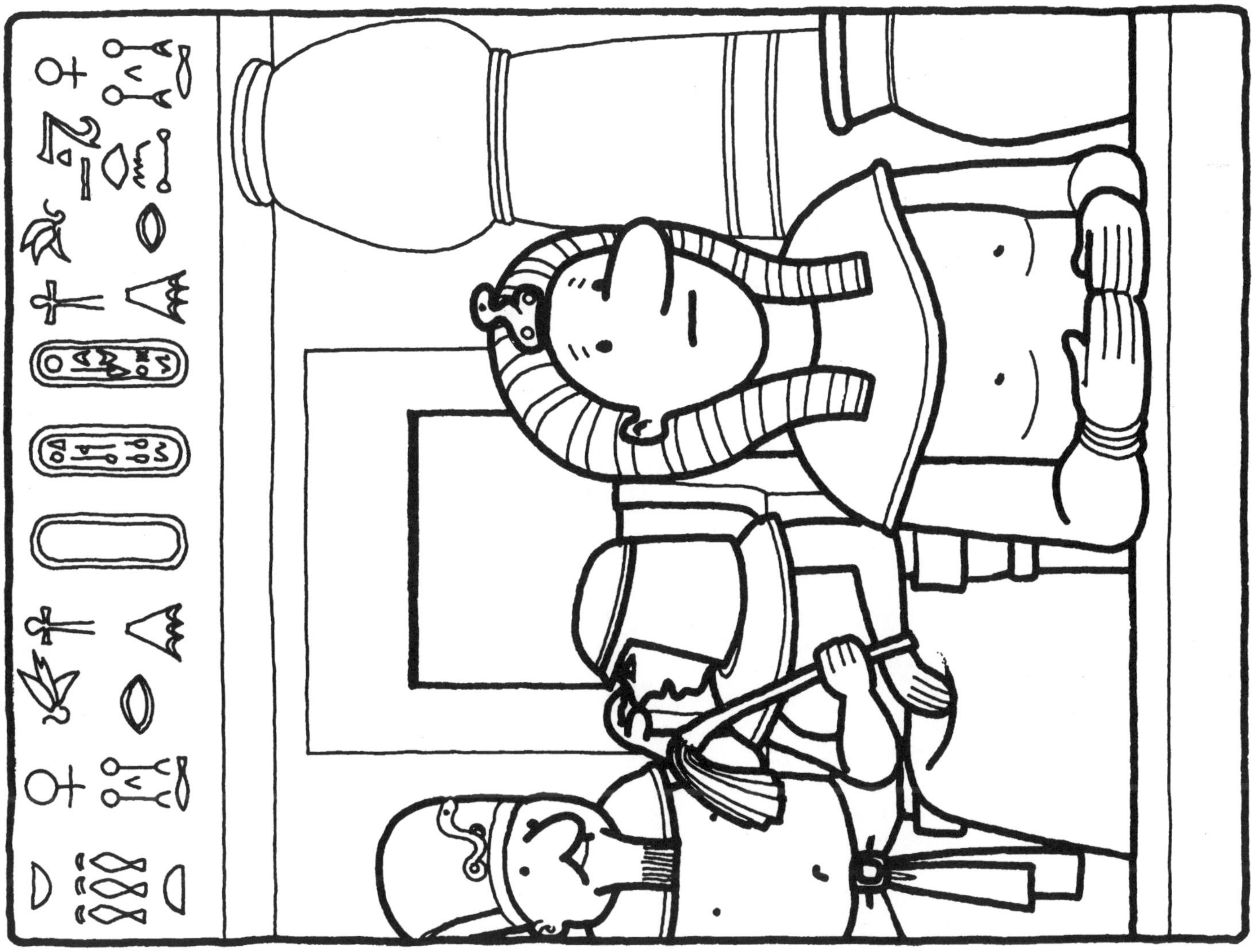

Ruth and Naomi

The full story is told in *Ruth and Naomi,*
ISBN 0 86209 506 9

After Mahlon and Chilion had died, Naomi, Orpah and Ruth went on a long journey to Judah, Naomi's old home.

On the way Naomi looked sadly at Ruth and Orpah and said, 'Oh dear, this is wrong, I shouldn't be taking you to my country. You should go back to your own families. They will find new husbands for you both.'

Orpah went back to her family but Ruth stayed with Naomi. When they reached Judah, all Naomi's friends and relations hurried out to greet them.

It was harvest time, so Ruth went into the fields to gather grain for bread. Boaz, the man who owned the fields, saw her and the workers told him all about Ruth and how she had refused to leave her mother-in-law's side.

Boaz decided to marry Ruth, so he gathered the ten leaders of the town to tell them.

Ruth and Boaz were married and they took Naomi to live with them in their new home.

Solomon's Secret

The full story is told in *Solomon's Secret*,
ISBN 0 86209 498 4

After the death of David, Solomon was made king. One night he heard God's voice say, 'Solomon, I will help you. What would you like me to give you?' Solomon said, 'I need to be really wise so that I can tell the difference between right and wrong.'

Solomon grew to be a very wise king. One day, two women came to the king with a baby. The first woman said, 'Not long ago we both give birth to baby boys. Hers was sick one night and died.'

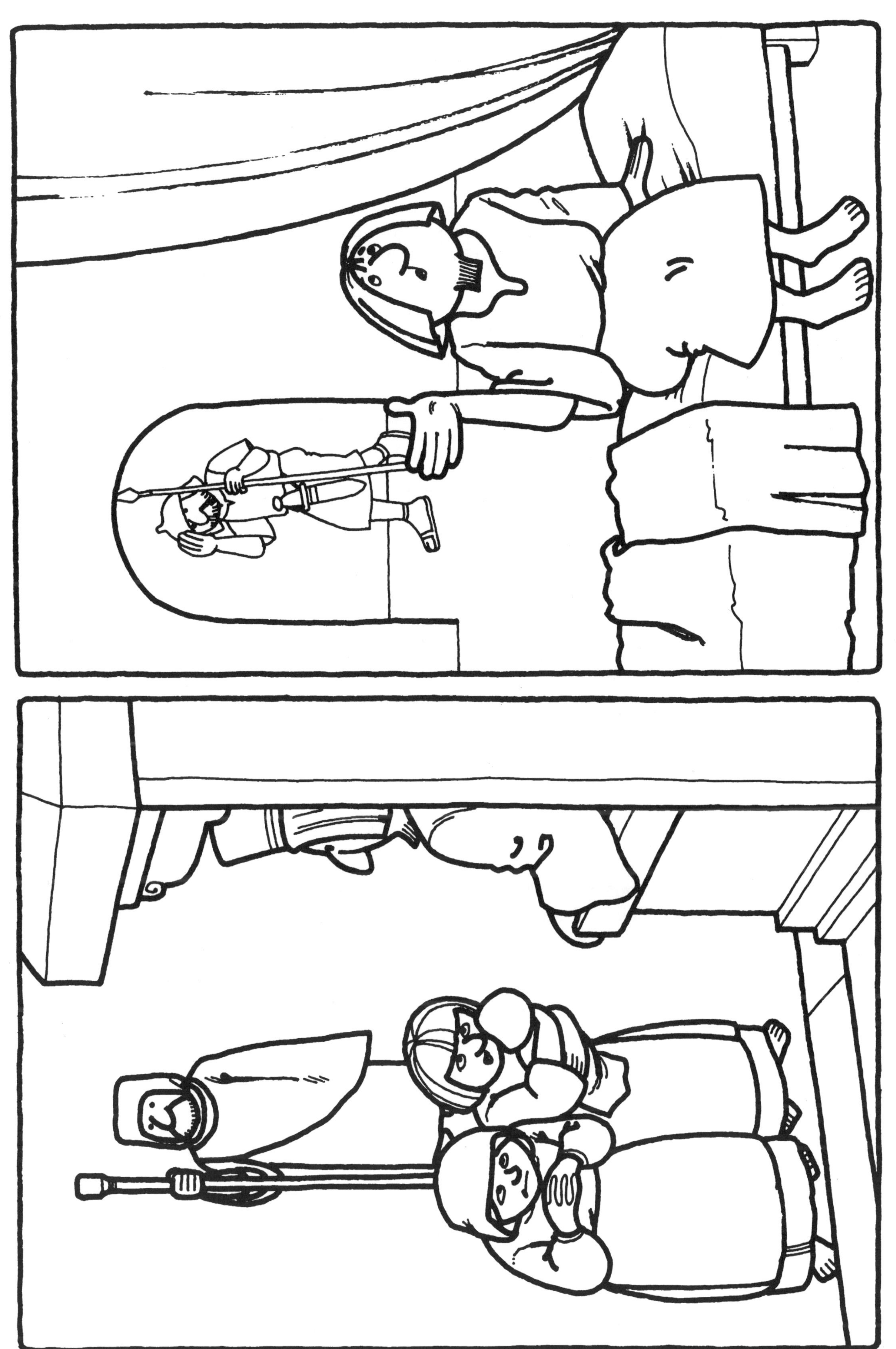

The first woman continued, 'Then she got up during the night while I was asleep and took my baby, putting hers in his place.'

'That's not true!' said the other woman, '*This* baby is mine; that dead one was yours!'

The two women shouted at each other. 'STOP!' ordered the king. 'Bring the baby here,' he said, 'and a sharp sword.' Then he turned to a soldier and said, 'I command you to cut the baby in two and give half to each woman.'

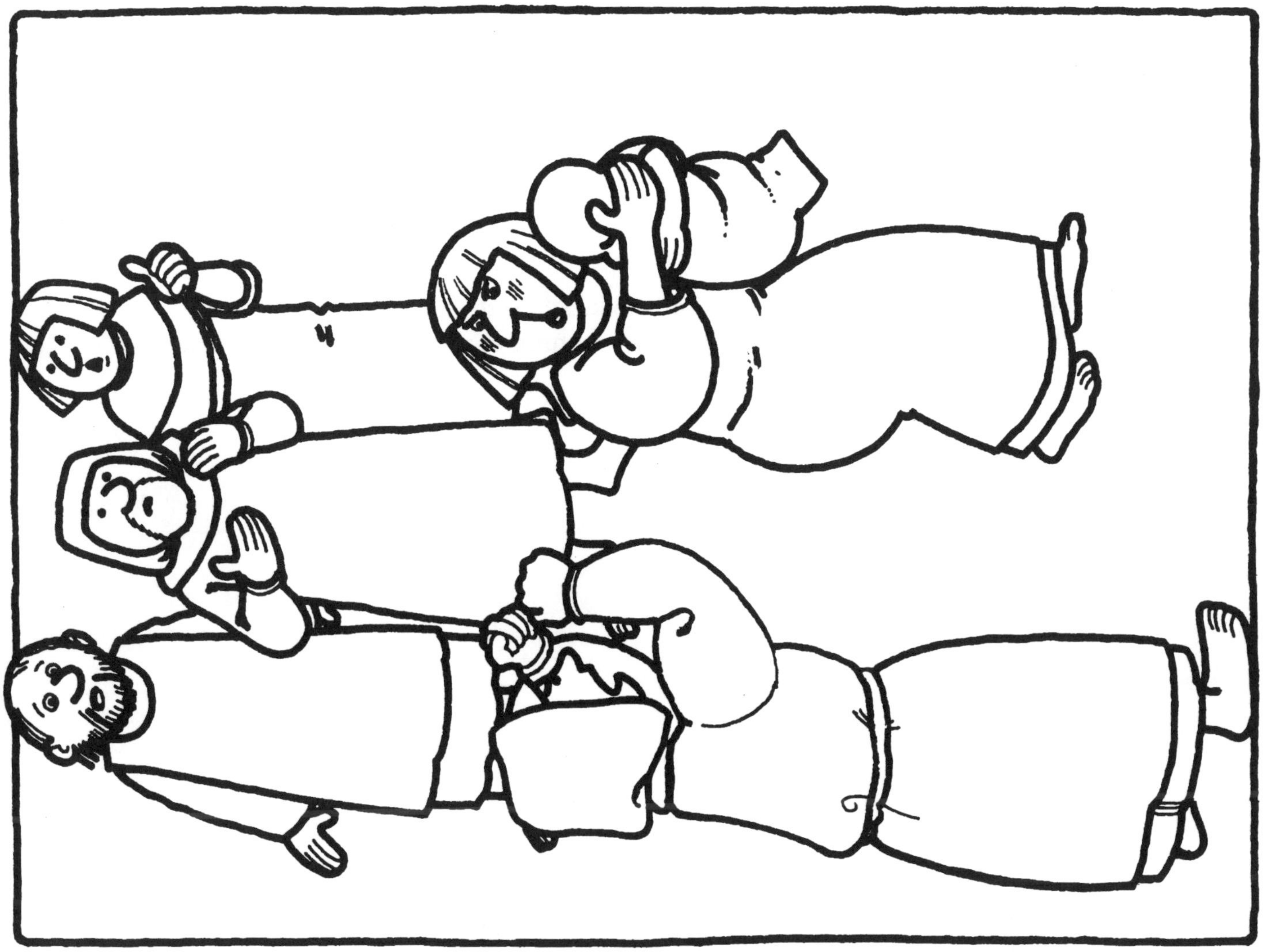

The real mother threw herself at the king's feet. 'No, no! Please don't kill him! She can have him, she can have him – but *please* don't kill him!'

'STOP!' he said. 'Don't kill the baby. Give it to this woman because she is the real mother.'

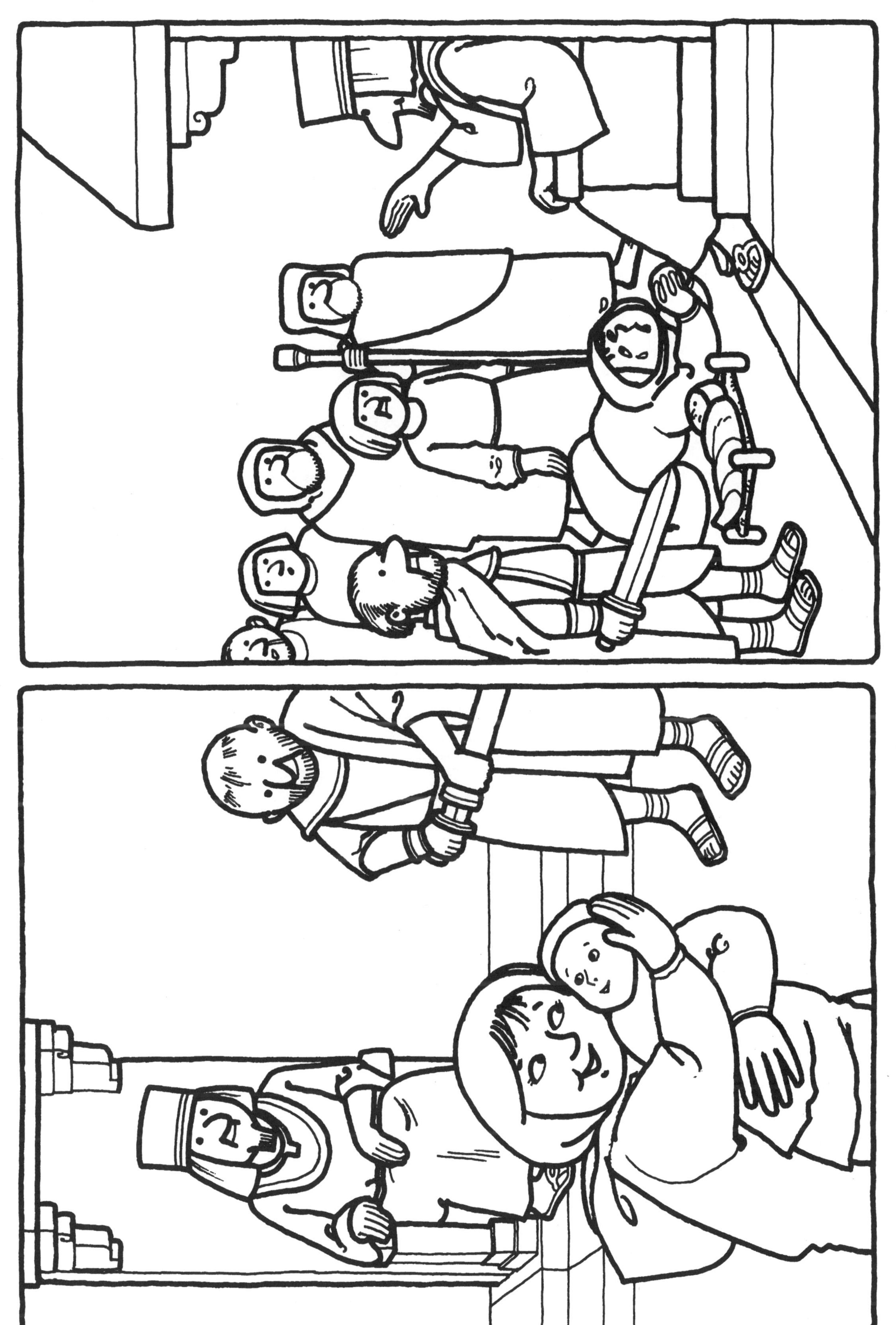

Daniel and the Lions

The full story is told in *Daniel and the Lions*,
ISBN 0 86209 358 9

Daniel lived in Babylon and was a good and kind man who loved God very much. Three times a day, he knelt at the window of his house and prayed to God.

King Darius called Daniel and said, 'Daniel, I want you to look after part of my kingdom for me.'

The people of Babylon did not believe in God. They prayed to statues. Some of them even prayed to King Darius! But Daniel knew it was wrong.

Not everybody liked Daniel. So they plotted to get rid of him. They told the king that everyone should pray to him alone for thirty days and that anyone who didn't should be thrown to the lions!

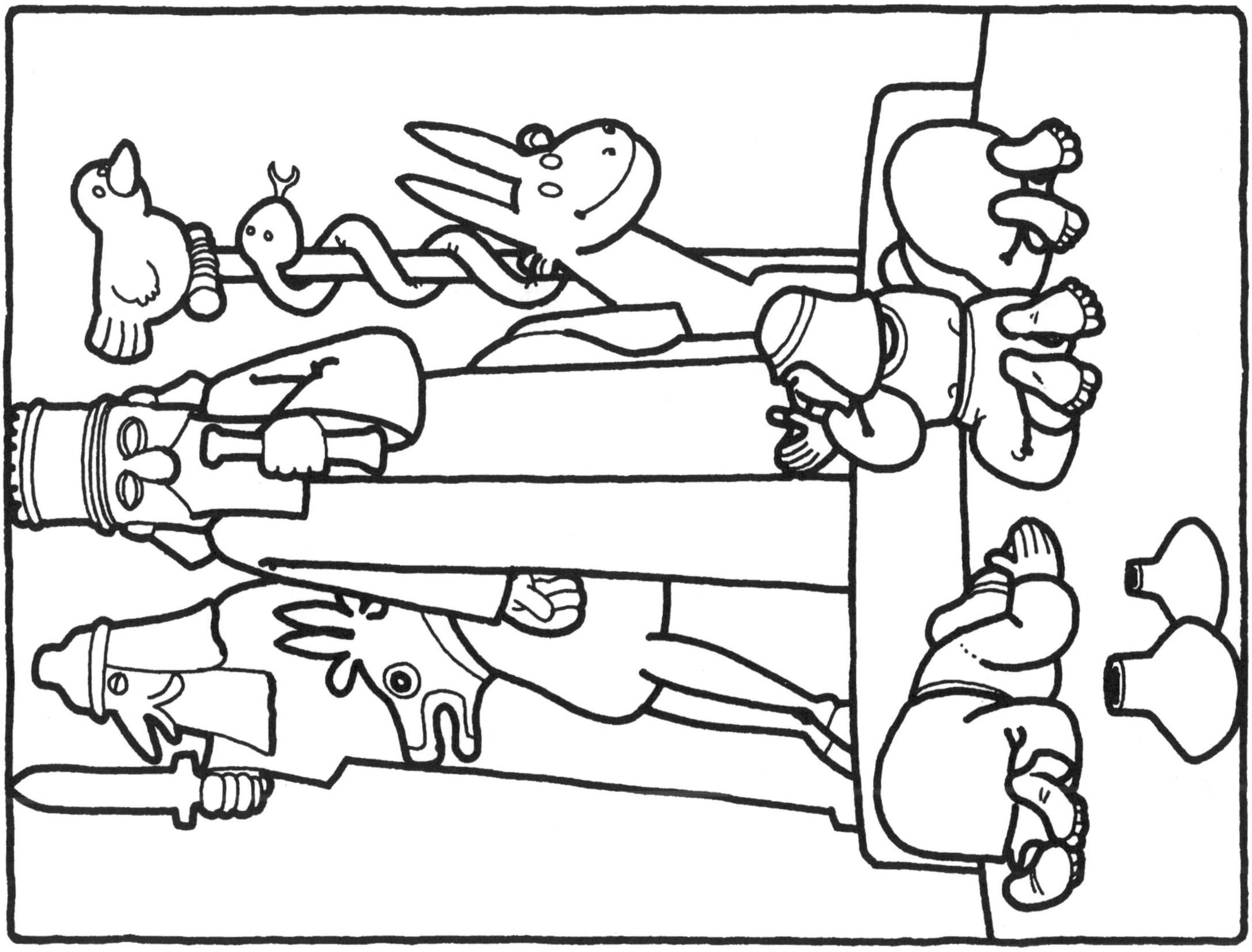

Daniel was arrested for not praying to the King. King Darius was very sad because he loved Daniel very much and knew that he'd been tricked.

Daniel was lowered into the lions' den. Then the stone was rolled across the entrance.

Very early the next morning King Darius hurried to the lions' den. The stone was rolled back and there was Daniel, alive and unharmed!

King Darius was so happy his friend was safe. He ordered the plotters to be arrested and then ordered that everyone should believe in Daniel's God, because he is the only true living God.

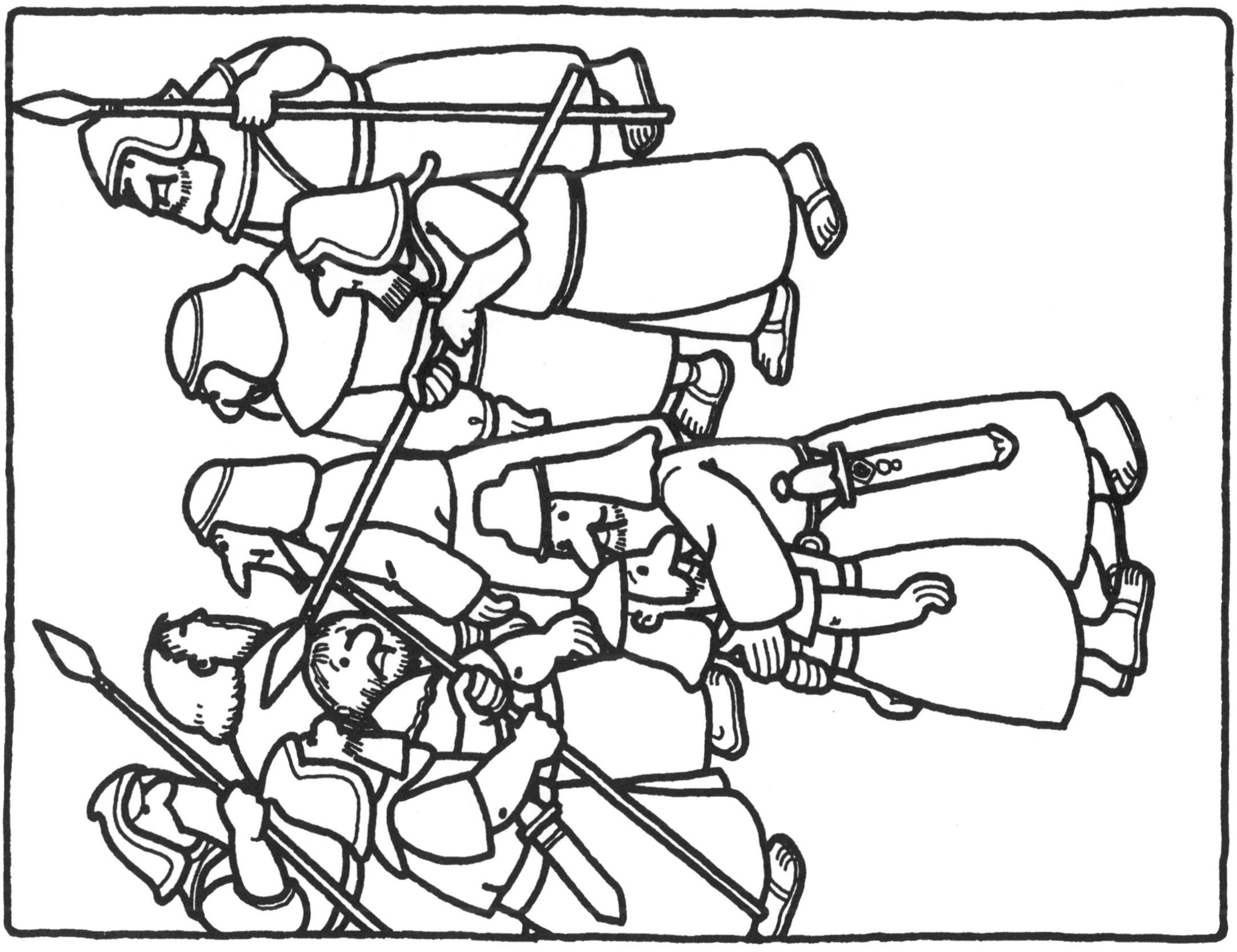

The Welcoming Party

The full story is told in *The Welcoming Party*,
ISBN 0 86209 426 7

Dog was rather important. When he heard that a baby had been born in Bethlehem, he set about organising a welcoming party, by telling all the animals.

The night was silent as the animals walked, hopped and flew to the stable where they sang to Jesus as an animal choir.

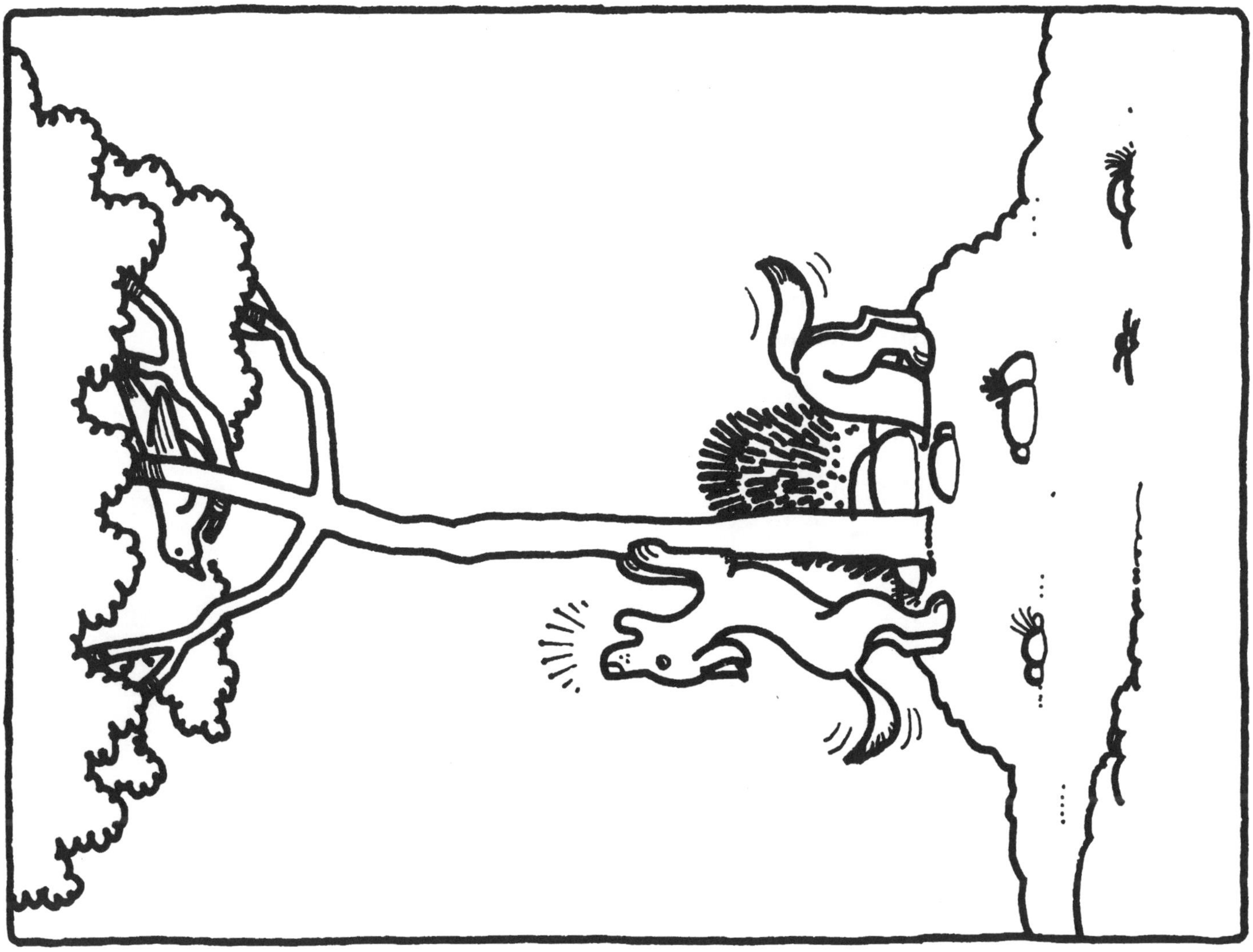

Then each animal sang a solo to greet the baby Jesus. Ox was first – after all, it was his stable they were using!

When the mouse sang, not even the cat scared him, it was such a peaceful night.

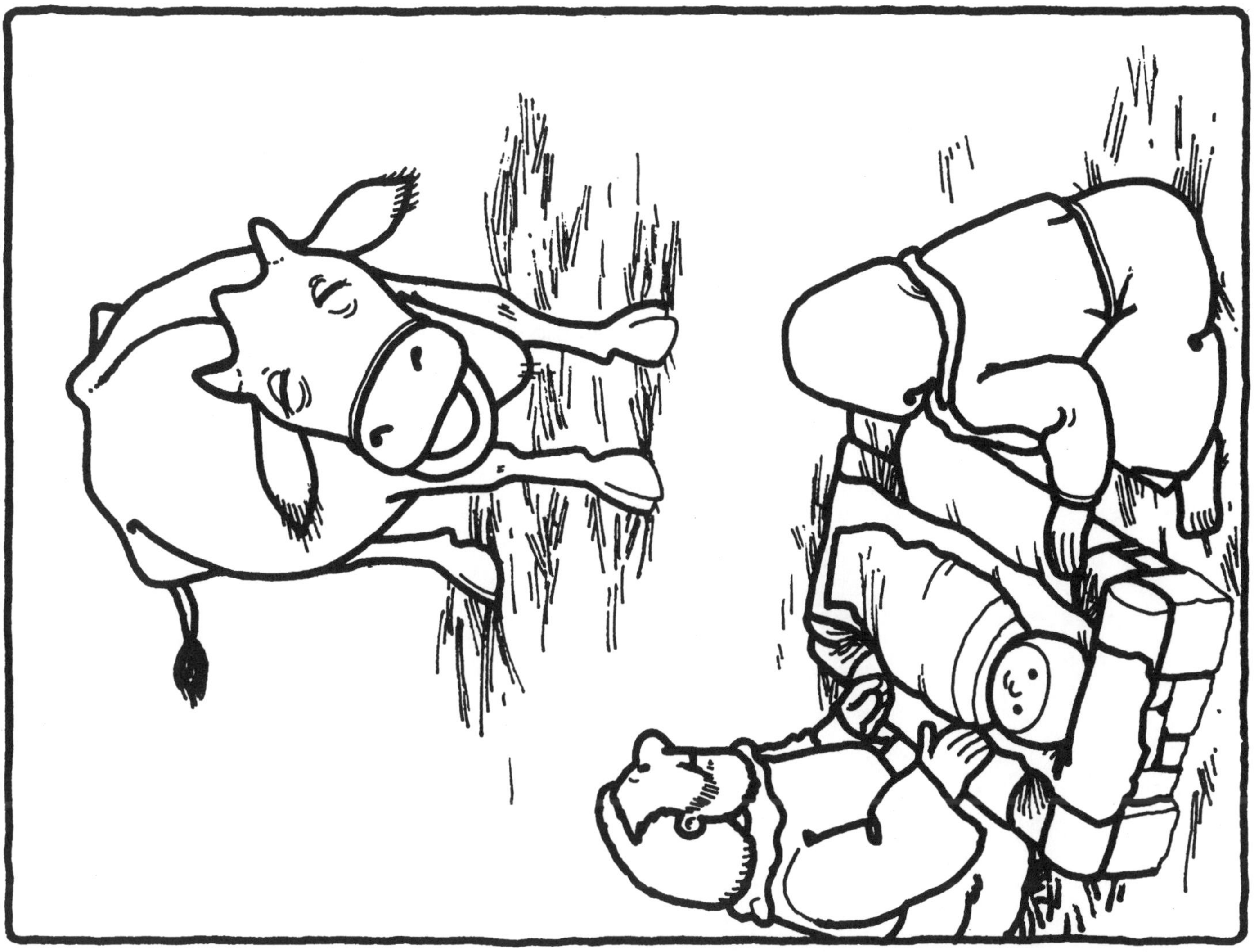

Just then the shepherds arrived from the hills, bringing their sheep with them. As soon as the sheep saw Jesus they broke into song as well!

Cat found herself a nice pile of straw underneath the stall where Jesus lay. She wasn't even interested in chasing mice, so she sang as well!

At last it was dog's turn and he decided to do something spectacular. He sang and he jumped and knocked the chicken off her perch!

The last to arrive were the camels, carrying the three wise men with their gifts for the baby. The camels were the last to sing. What a wonderful welcoming party it was!

Jesus Gets Lost

The full story is told in *Jesus Gets Lost,*
ISBN 0 86209 509 3

Joseph was the village carpenter and Jesus loved to help him.

Each year everyone in the village went to the big city called Jerusalem. They went for one of the most important Jewish feasts – the feast of the Passover.

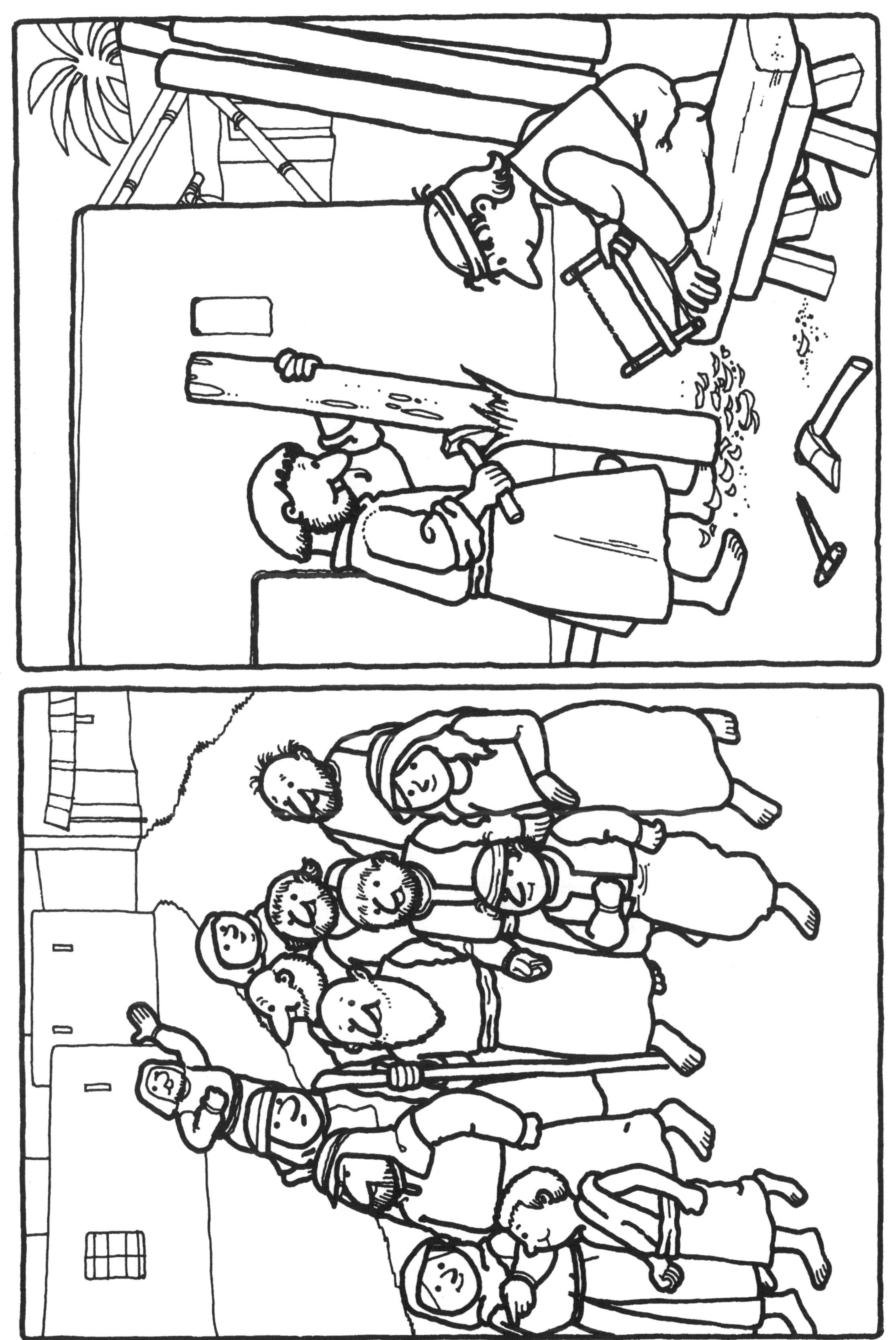

After visiting the temple, Joseph, Mary and Jesus decided to look around the shops.

At last it was time to leave, but Jesus was not with them! So Mary and Joseph made their way back to Jerusalem to look for him.

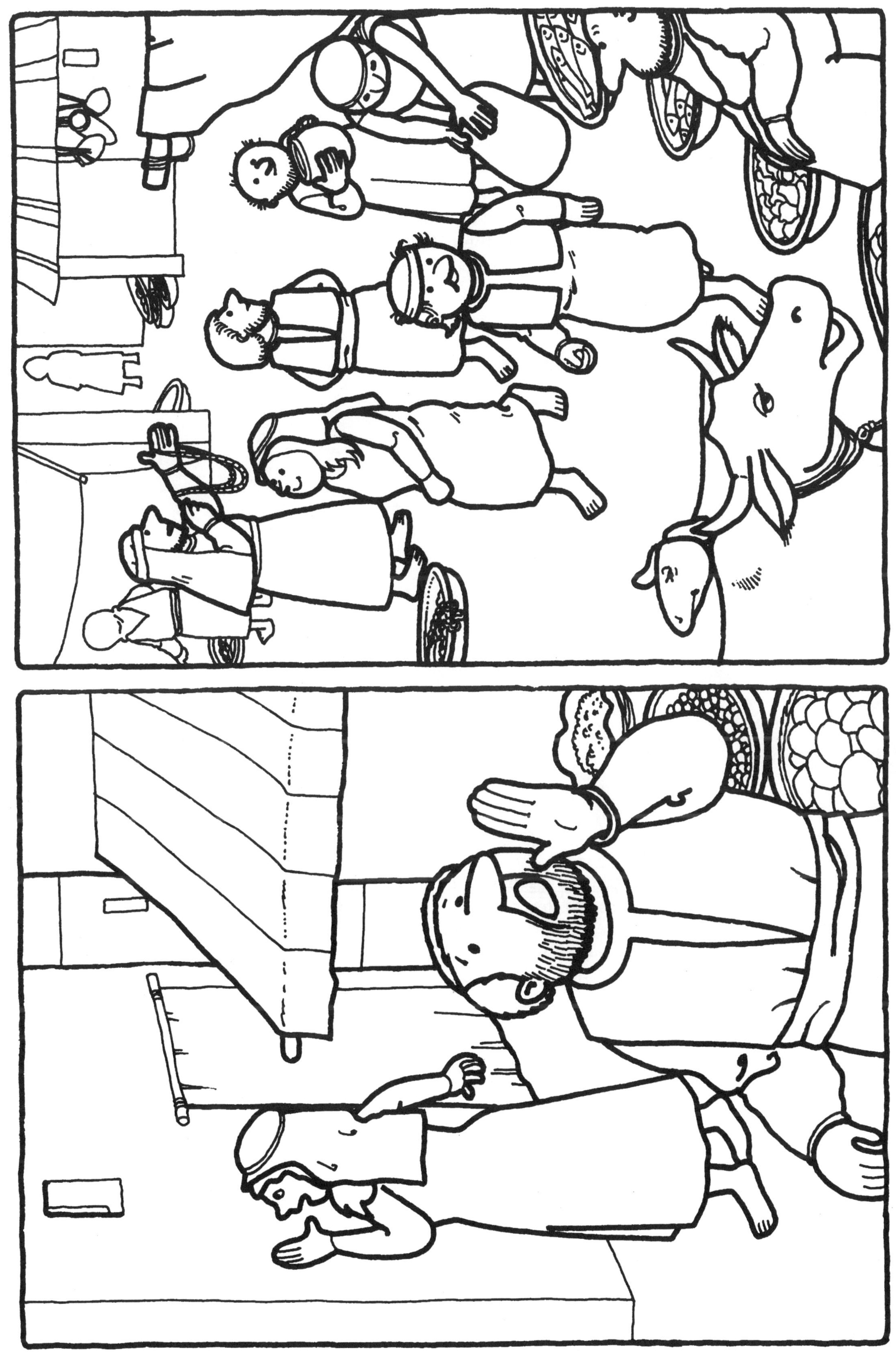

Mary and Joseph noticed crowds making their way to the temple, so they joined them. Jesus was in the temple, with the Jewish teachers, called rabbis.

Mary and Joseph were relieved to find Jesus, but were a little cross too. Jesus said to them, 'Why did you worry so much? You know I must do the work of my Father in heaven.' After this, they made their way back to Nazareth, glad to have Jesus safe with them again.

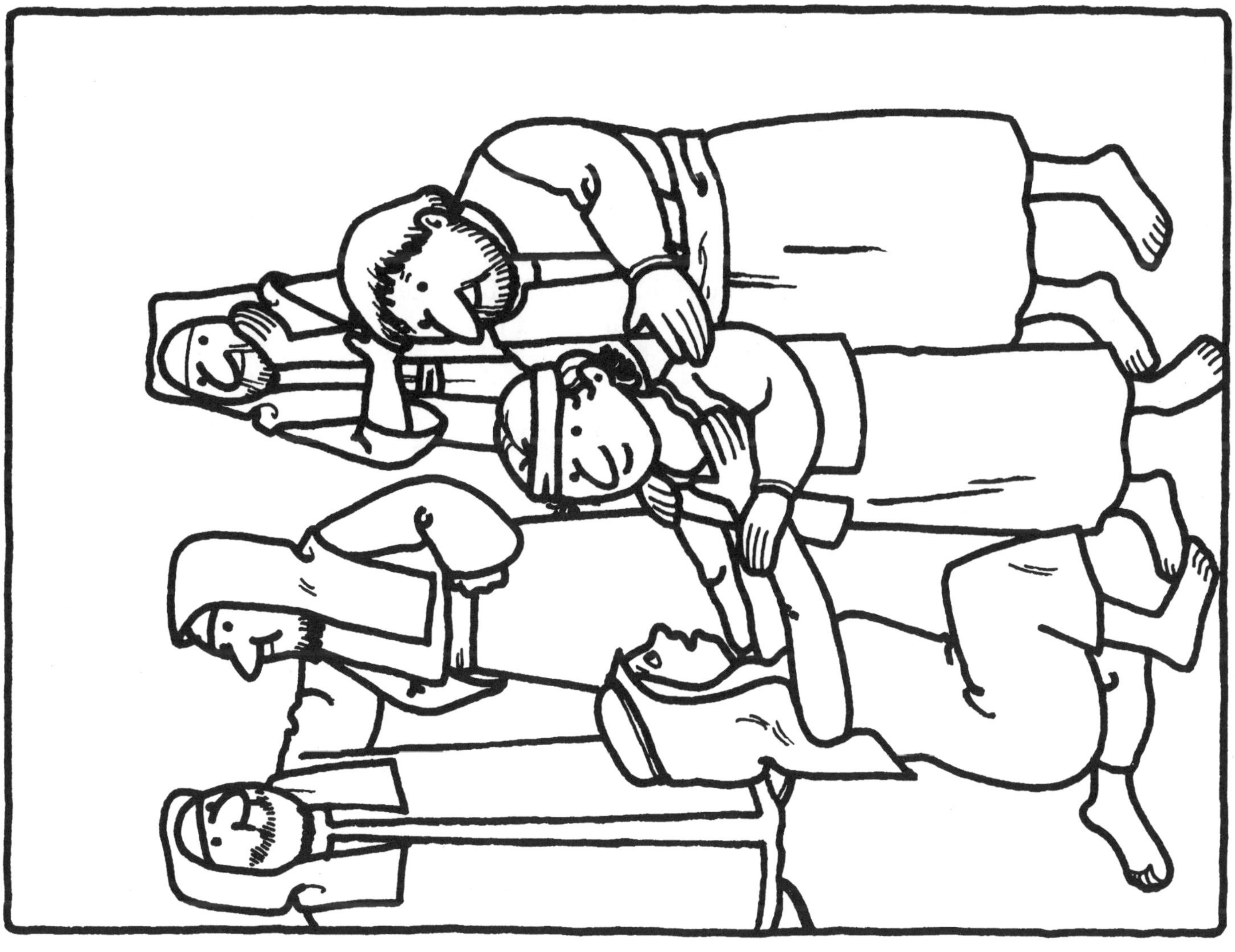

The Soldier Who Gave Orders

The full story is told in *The Soldier Who Gave Orders*,
ISBN 0 86209 427 5

Quentus was a centurion who gave orders and got things done.

One day his servant Festin fell ill. As Festin didn't get better, Quentus had an idea. A man called Jesus was visiting Capernaum and he was good at making people well again.

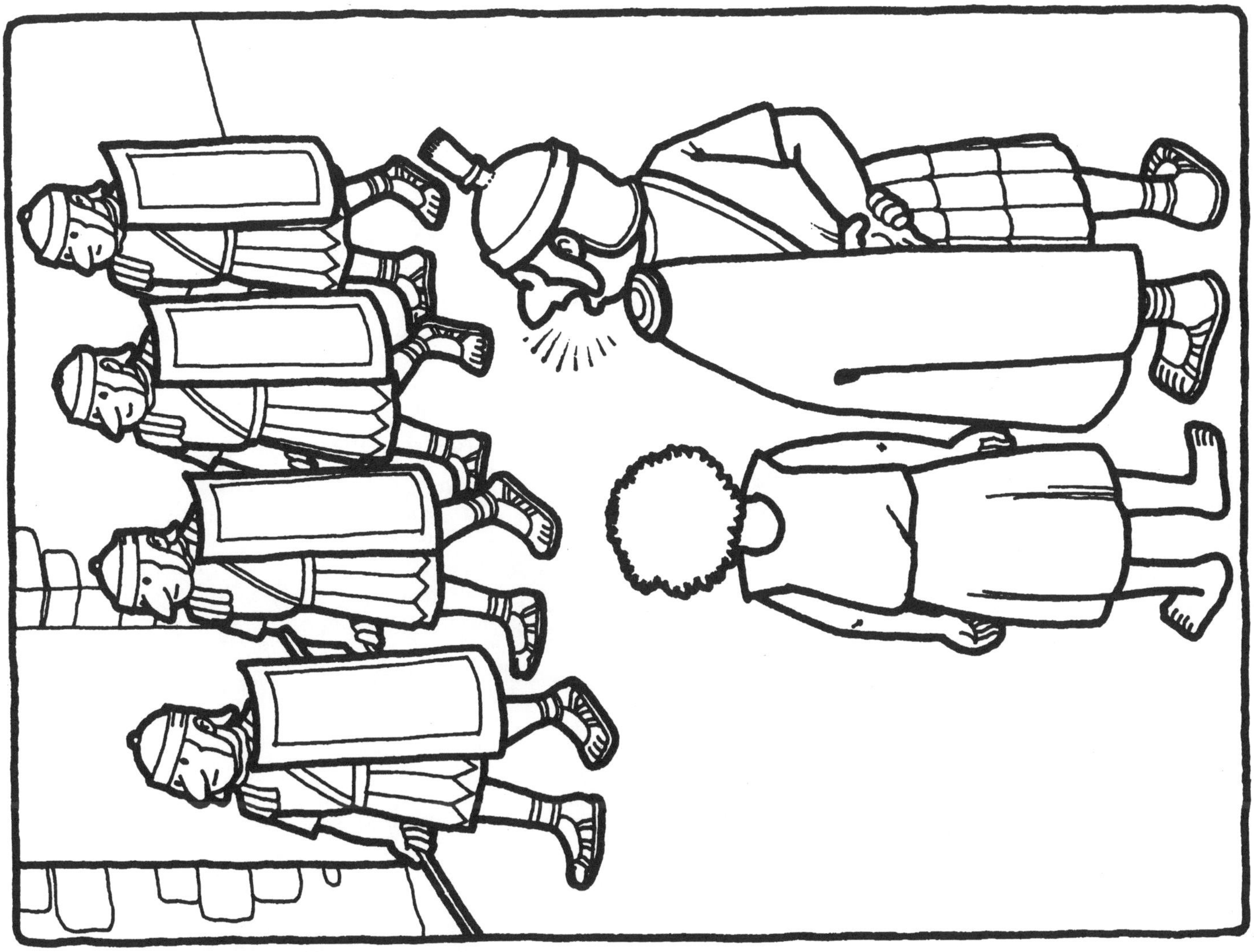

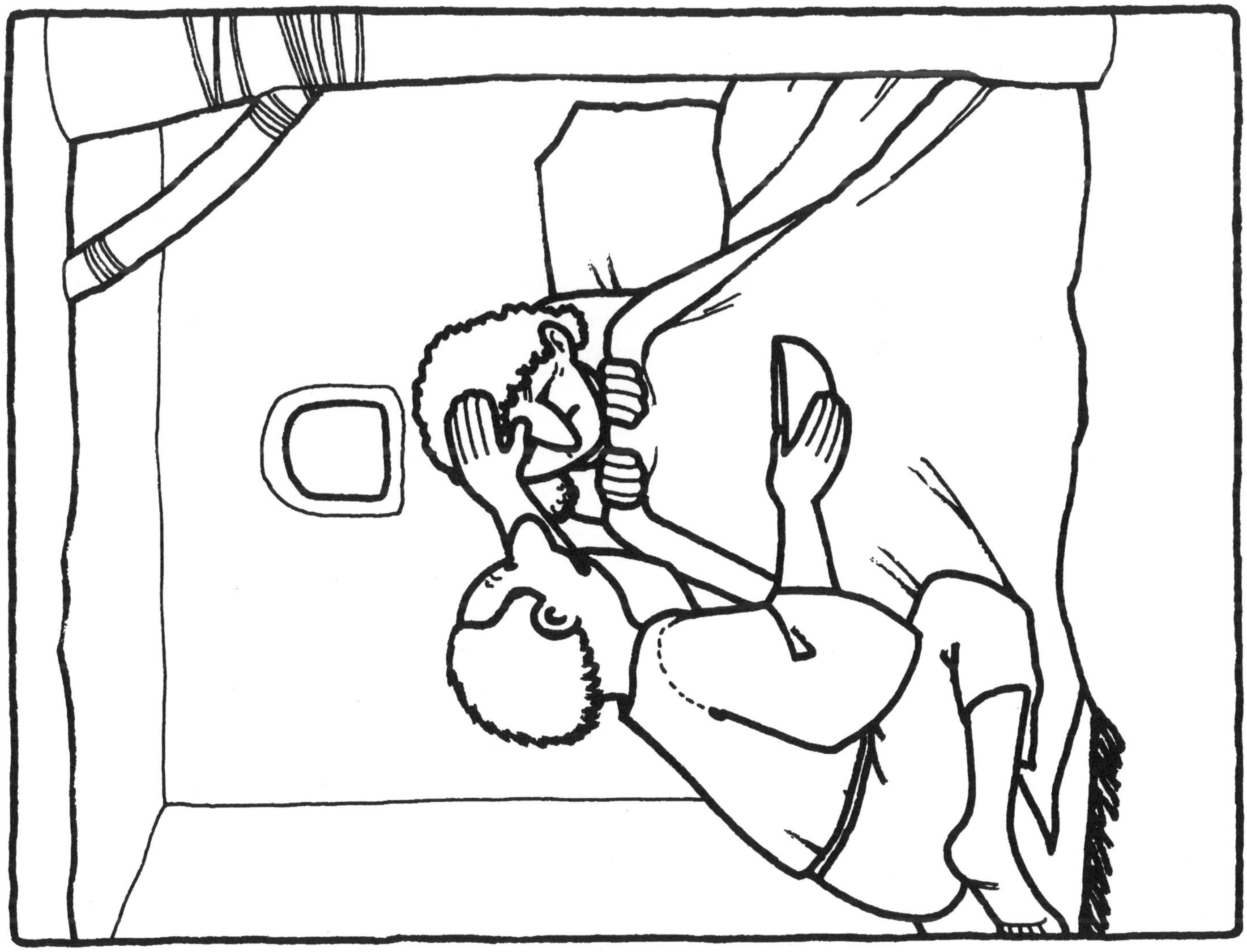

Quentus said to Jesus, 'My young servant can't move and is in terrible pain.'

'Then I will heal him,' said Jesus.

'Sir, I am a soldier and used to orders, and you have more power than I. If you just give the order I know my servant will be healed.'

Jesus was amazed. 'I have never met anyone who trusts me so much! Go home now. Let your servant be healed, just as you believed he would be.'

Quentus ran home and found his servant well. His illness had vanished.

Quentus was so pleased that he took his servant to see Jesus. 'There is the man who made you better,' he said.

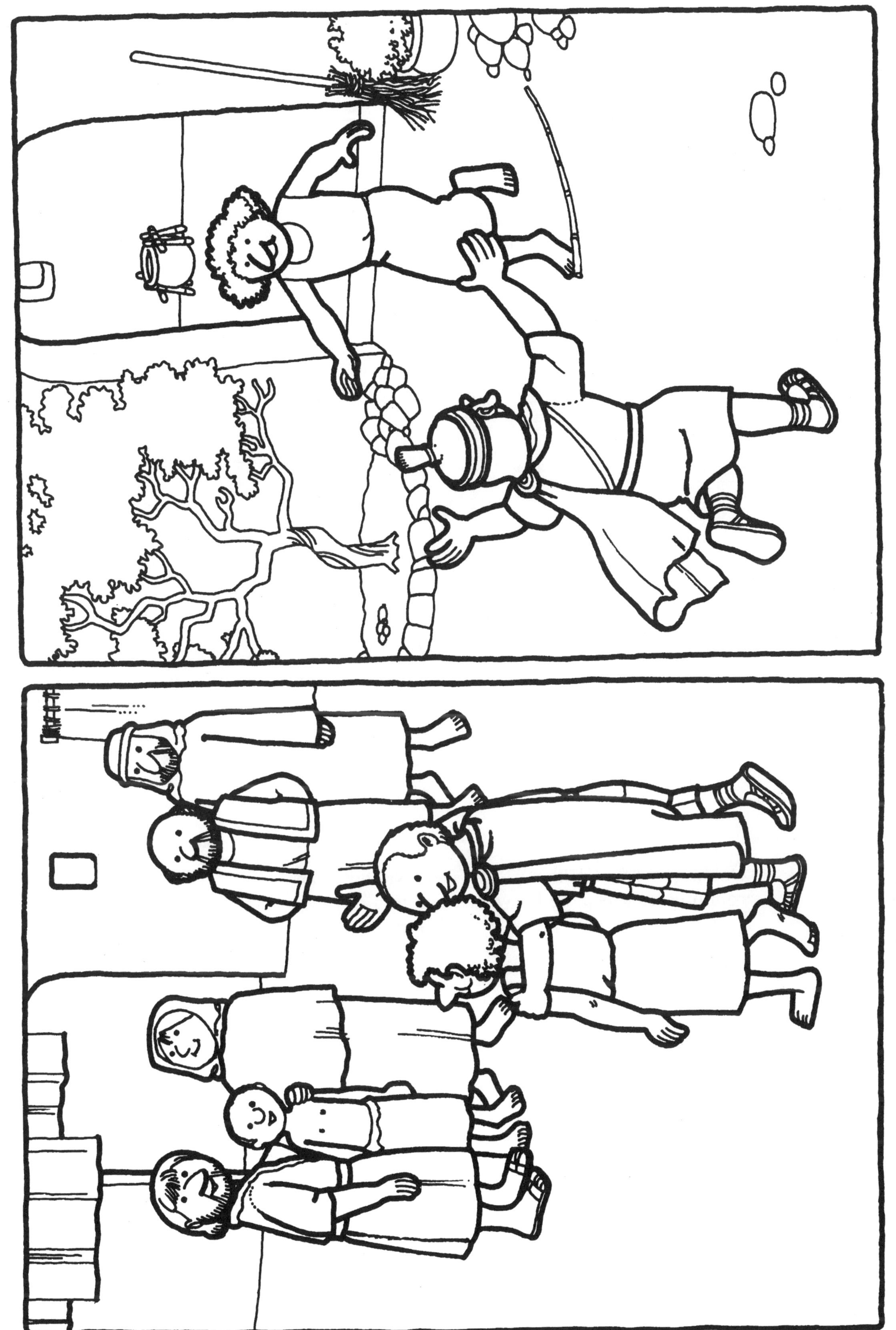

The Lost Sheep

The full story is told in *The Lost Sheep;*
ISBN 0 86209 508 5

This is a story that Jesus told. There once was a shepherd called Ezra, and his pride and joy were his sheep. Because he loved them all, he gave each one a name.

One day, a dreadful thing happened. Without even counting his sheep, he knew that one was missing. Very quickly he realised that it was Henry.

Without even stopping to think, Ezra grabbed his walking stick and set off to look for Henry. At that moment, Henry was all that mattered to him. The other sheep could take care of themselves for now.

At last, a long, long way away, he saw . . . Henry, the lost sheep.

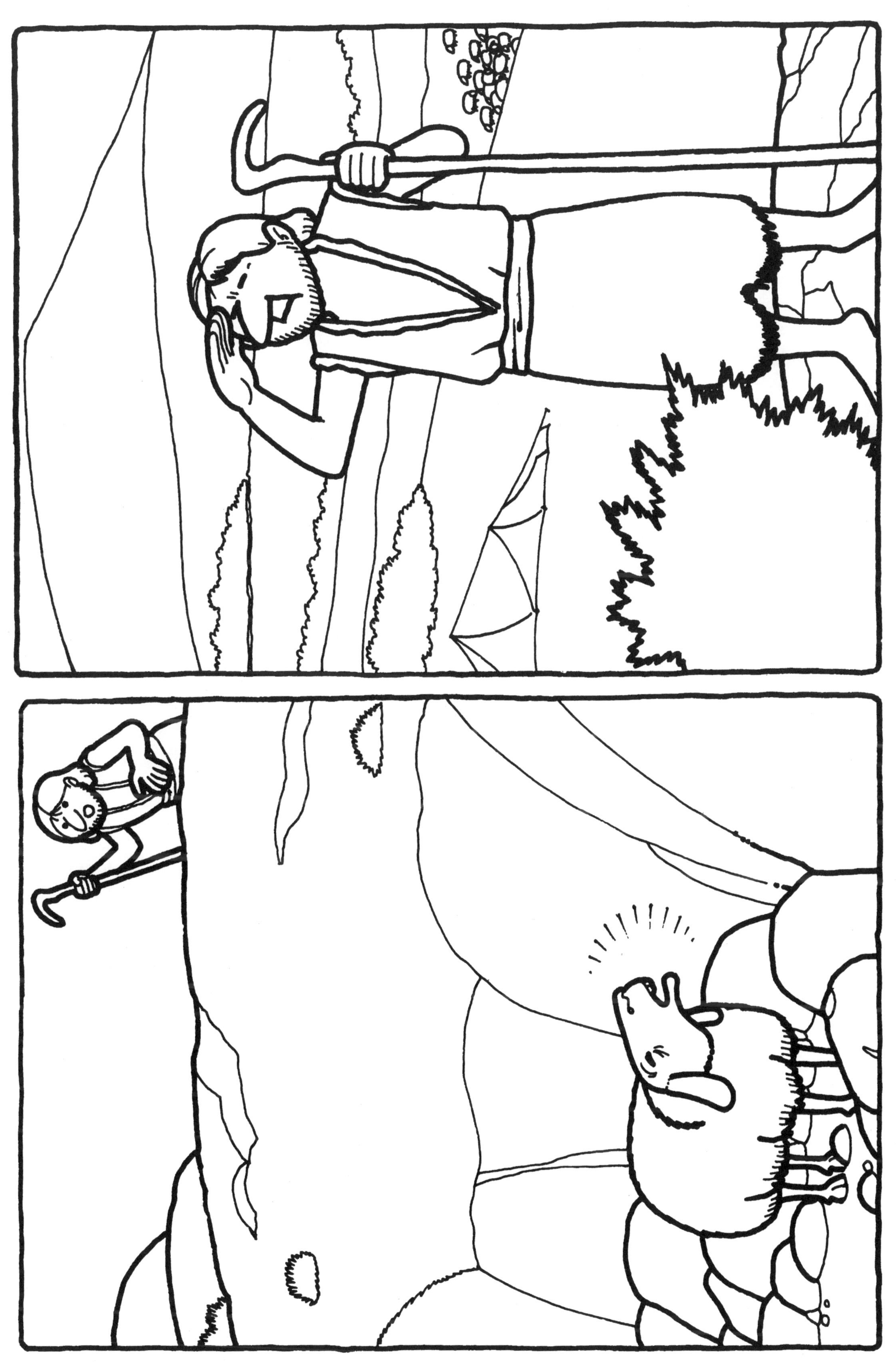

Ezra lifted Henry onto his shoulders and set off for home, shouting to everyone he met, 'I had lost one of my sheep, but now I have found him.'

When they came to the field, all the other sheep were waiting to say hello to Henry.

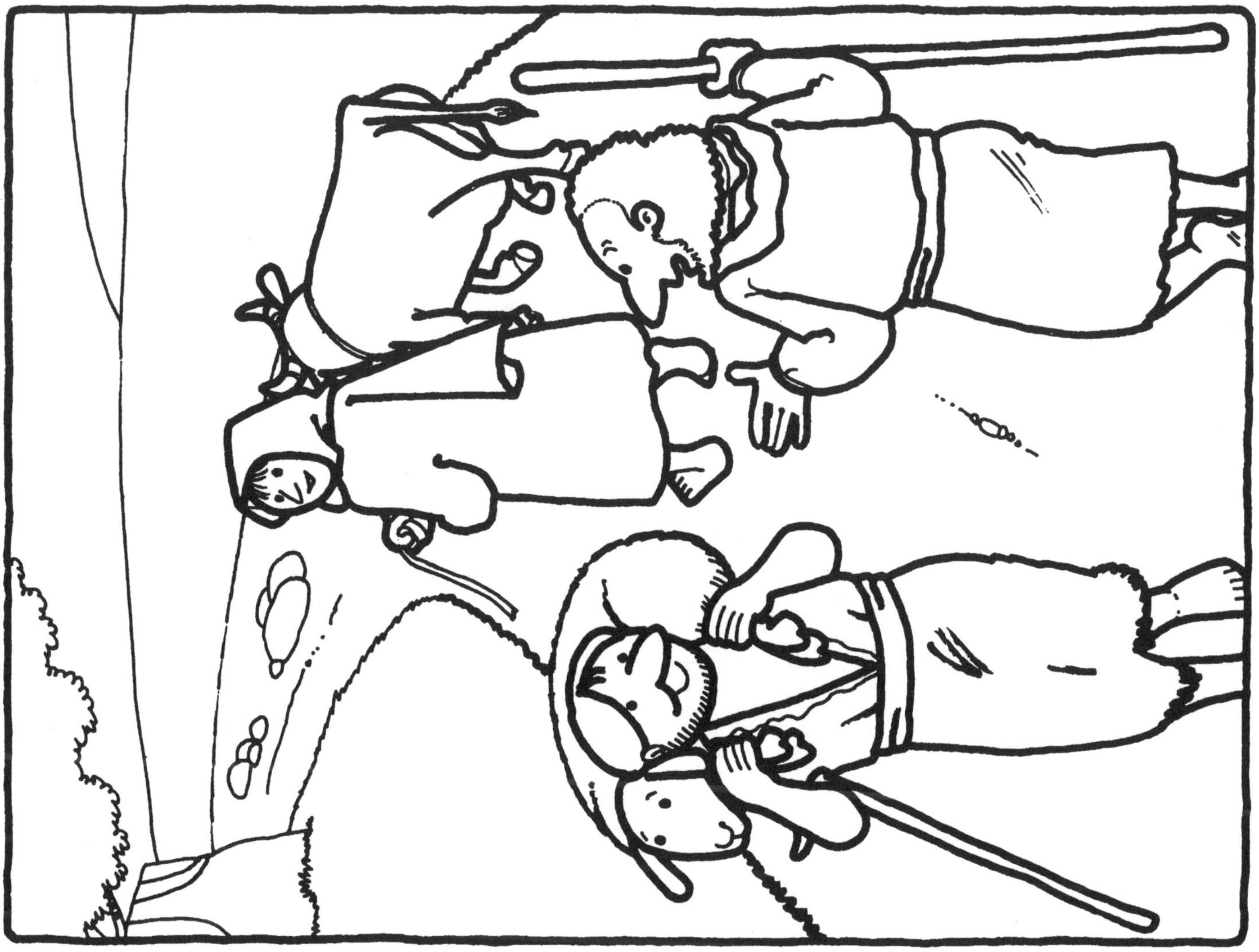

Ezra was so happy he decided to give a big party.

Jesus went on to explain that we are all like sheep and that our Father in heaven is our shepherd. And just as Ezra loved all his sheep, our Father in heaven loves each one of us very, very much.

Zacchaeus and Jesus

The full story is told in *Zacchaeus and Jesus*,
ISBN 0 86209 522 0

Zacchaeus was a tax collector. He lived in a very fine house on the edge of a town called Jericho. He had everything he could wish for, but had no friends.

One day, while collecting taxes, he overheard some women talking: 'They say Jesus, the miracle worker, is heading this way.'

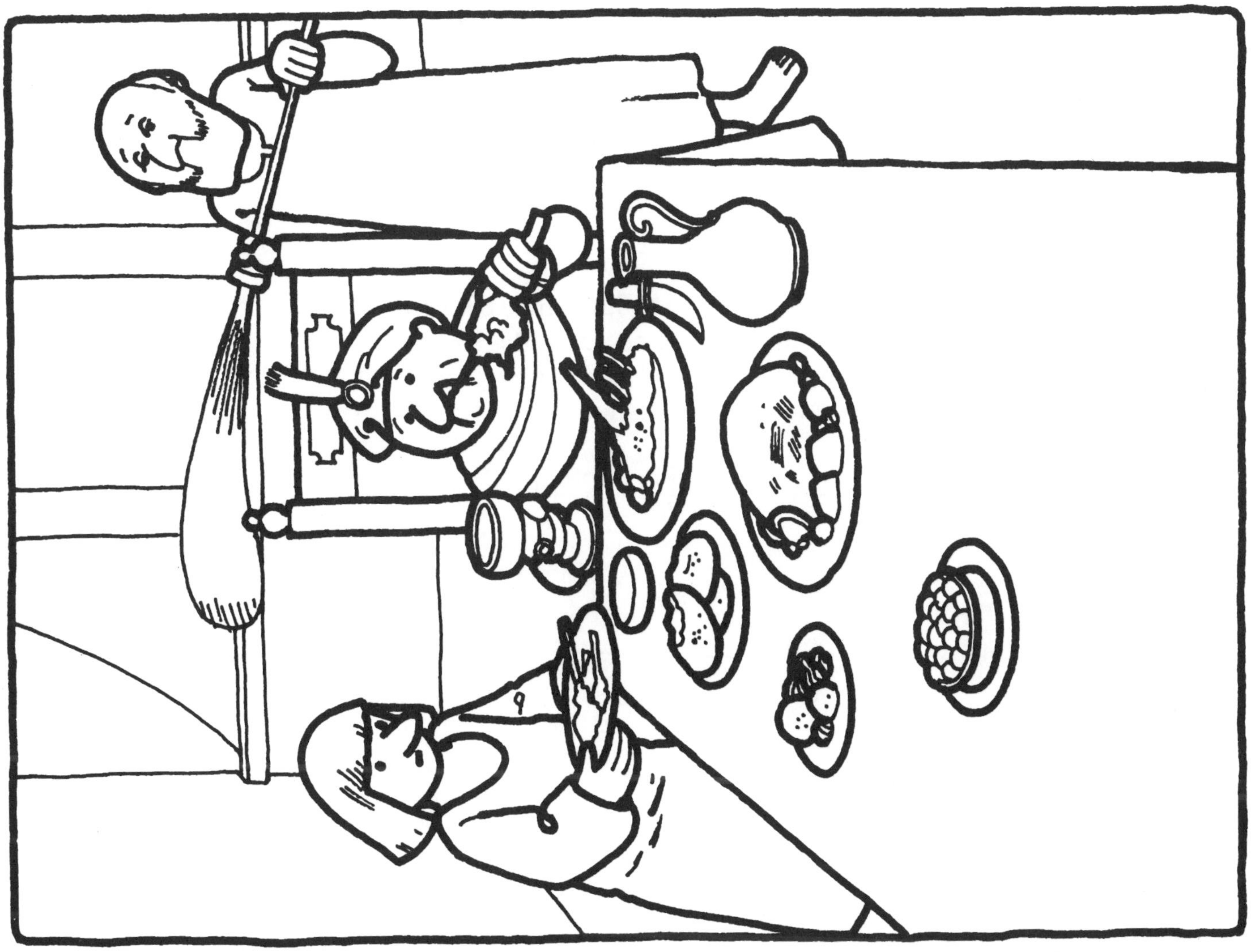

Zacchaeus decided to go and see him, and, because he was small, climbed a tree to see above the crowd! Jesus looked up and saw him and said, 'Hurry down, Zacchaeus, I'm coming to your house for a meal tonight.'

Zacchaeus jumped out of the tree and pushed his way through the crowd towards Jesus. He was so excited – at last, someone was coming to visit him at his home.

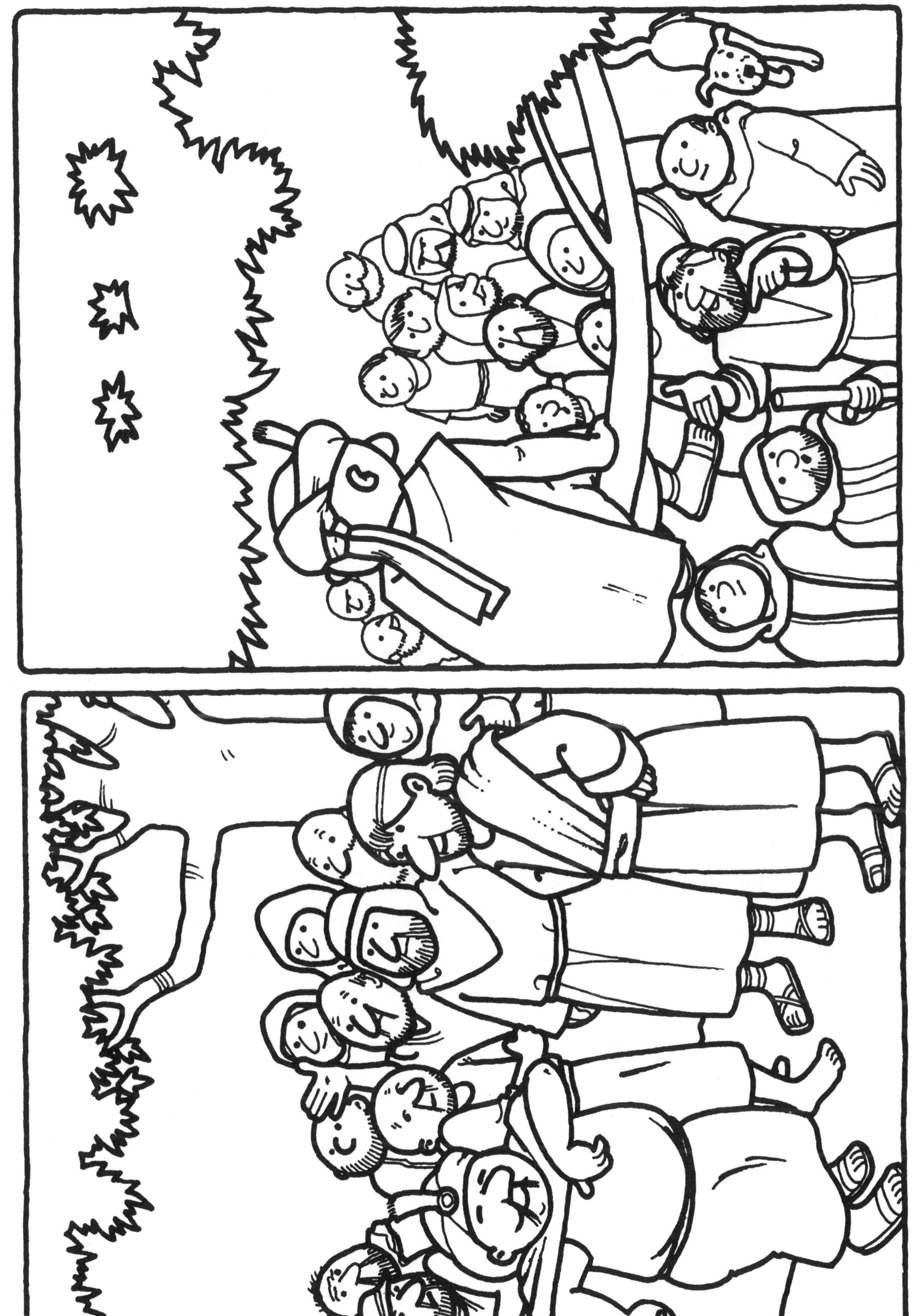

The people in the crowd grumbled to each other: 'Jesus shouldn't eat with the likes of Zacchaeus – he's a cheat and a liar.'

Jesus' visit meant so much to Zacchaeus that he decided to live a new life from that moment on. He gave half of everything he owned to the poor, and whoever he had cheated, he paid back four times as much!

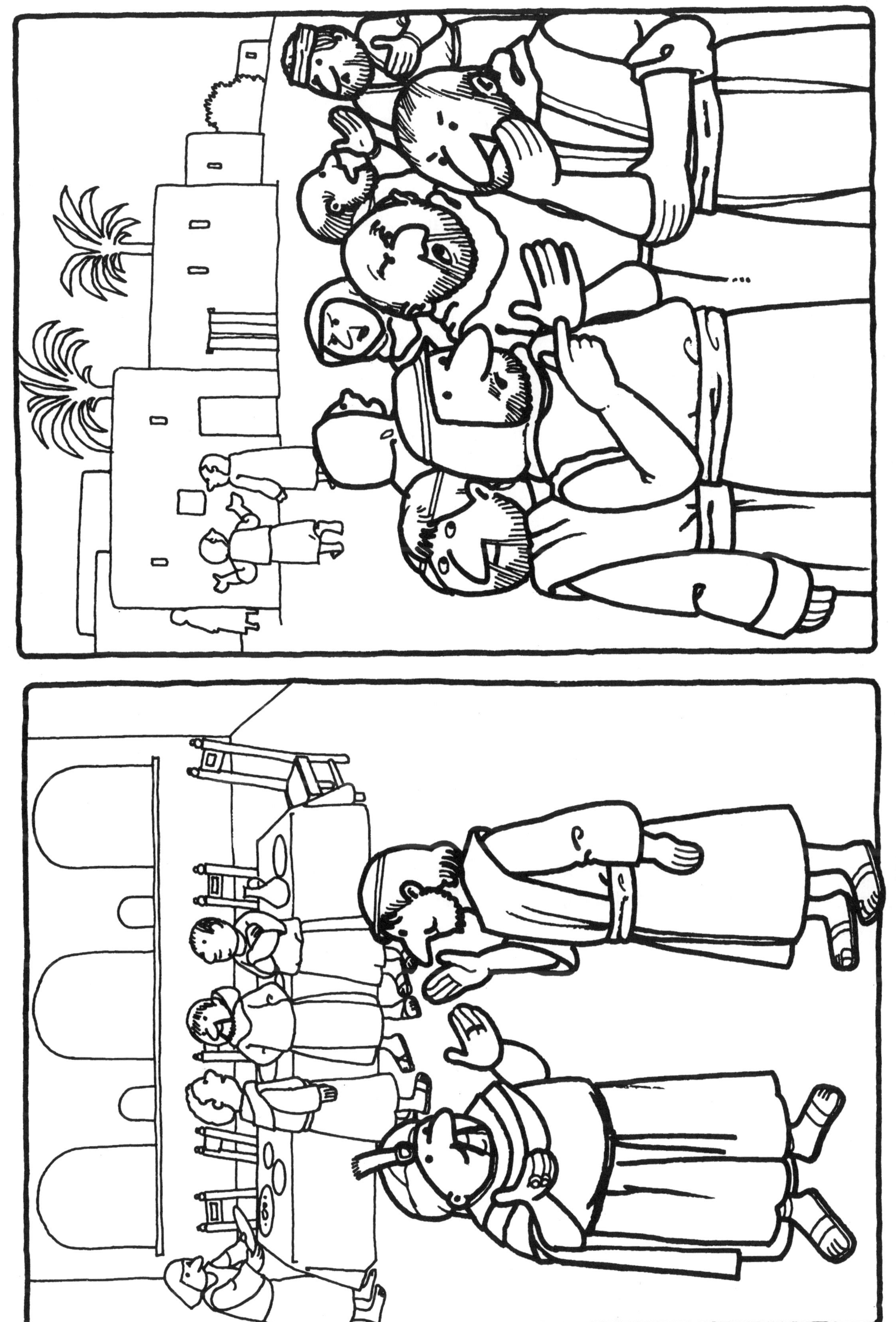

Five Loaves and Two Fish

The full story is told in *Five Loaves and Two Fish*,
ISBN 0 86209 361 9

Two children playing by Lake Galilee saw a fishing boat coming in to shore. They didn't seem to have caught any fish.

It was Jesus who had come ashore. He was talking to the people and telling them wise stories.

Jesus spoke to Philip, a disciple: 'Where can we get food for these people?'

A boy went to the disciple, Andrew. 'Please, sir,' he said, 'we have five loaves and two fish you can have.'

Jesus took the bread, thanked God for providing it, broke it into pieces, and handed it round. The bread and fish never ran out and others who had brought food began sharing it too.

When everyone had eaten, Jesus told his disciples to collect up the remains. There were twelve baskets full!

The Road to the Cross

The full story is told in *The Road to the Cross*,
ISBN 0 86209 368 6

At their Passover meal Jesus gave his friends bread and wine. 'I am giving you myself to set you free from all that is bad and wrong.' Then he said, 'One of you will hand me over to be killed.' No one believed him, including Peter. Jesus told him, 'Before the cock crows you will have let me down three times.'

After praying in the garden, Jesus was arrested by soldiers led to him by Judas, who greeted him with a kiss.

Peter denied knowing Jesus three times, and then the cock crowed. Jesus turned, and looked at Peter. You can guess how Peter felt.

Then Jesus was taken to the Roman governor, Pilate. The crowd shouted, 'Crucify him!'

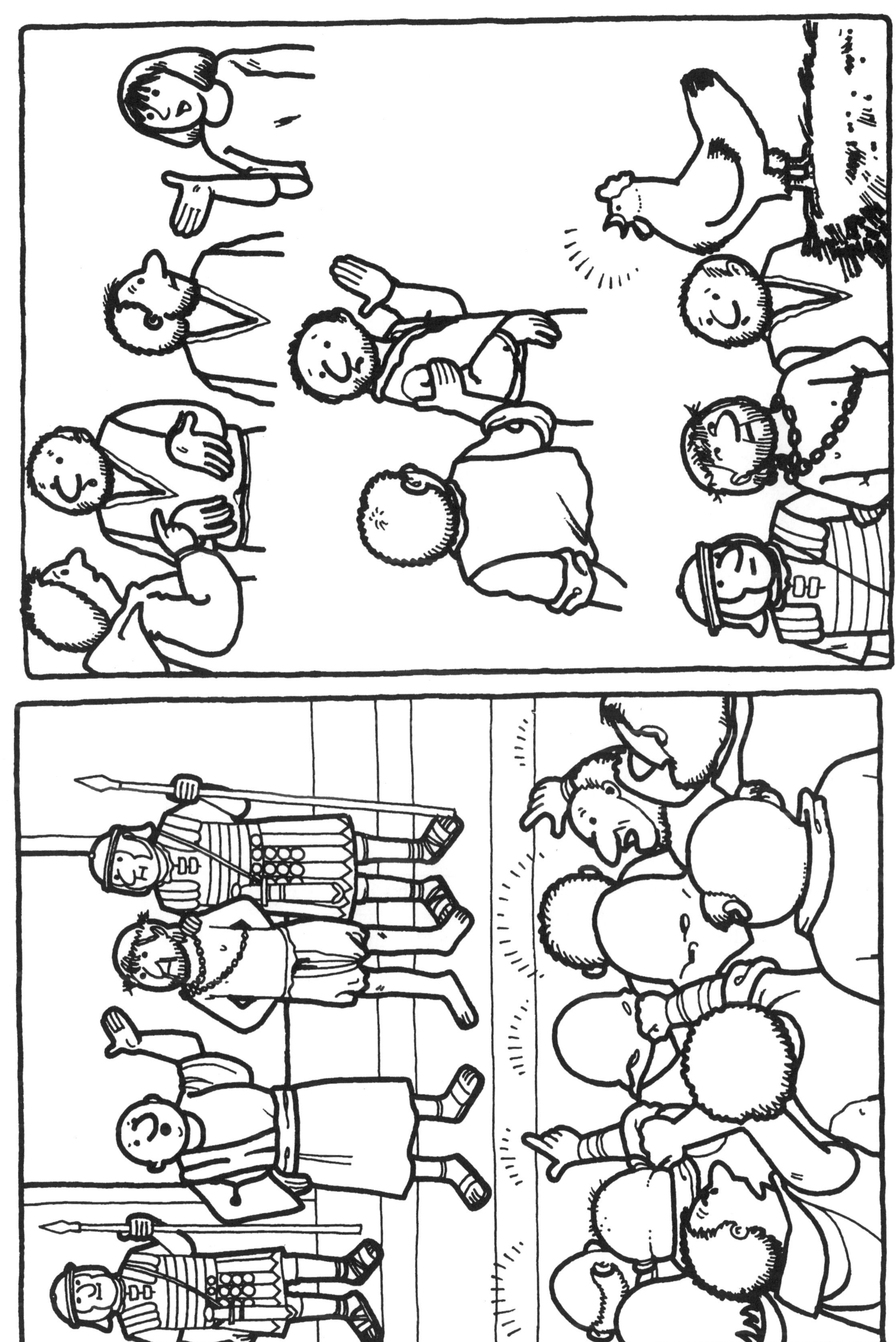

Jesus was crucified on a hill with two robbers. 'Father, forgive them,' he prayed; 'they don't understand what they are doing.'

When Jesus had died, his friends laid his body in a cave. It seemed like the end of everything. But it wasn't the end. A few days later Jesus would be alive again!

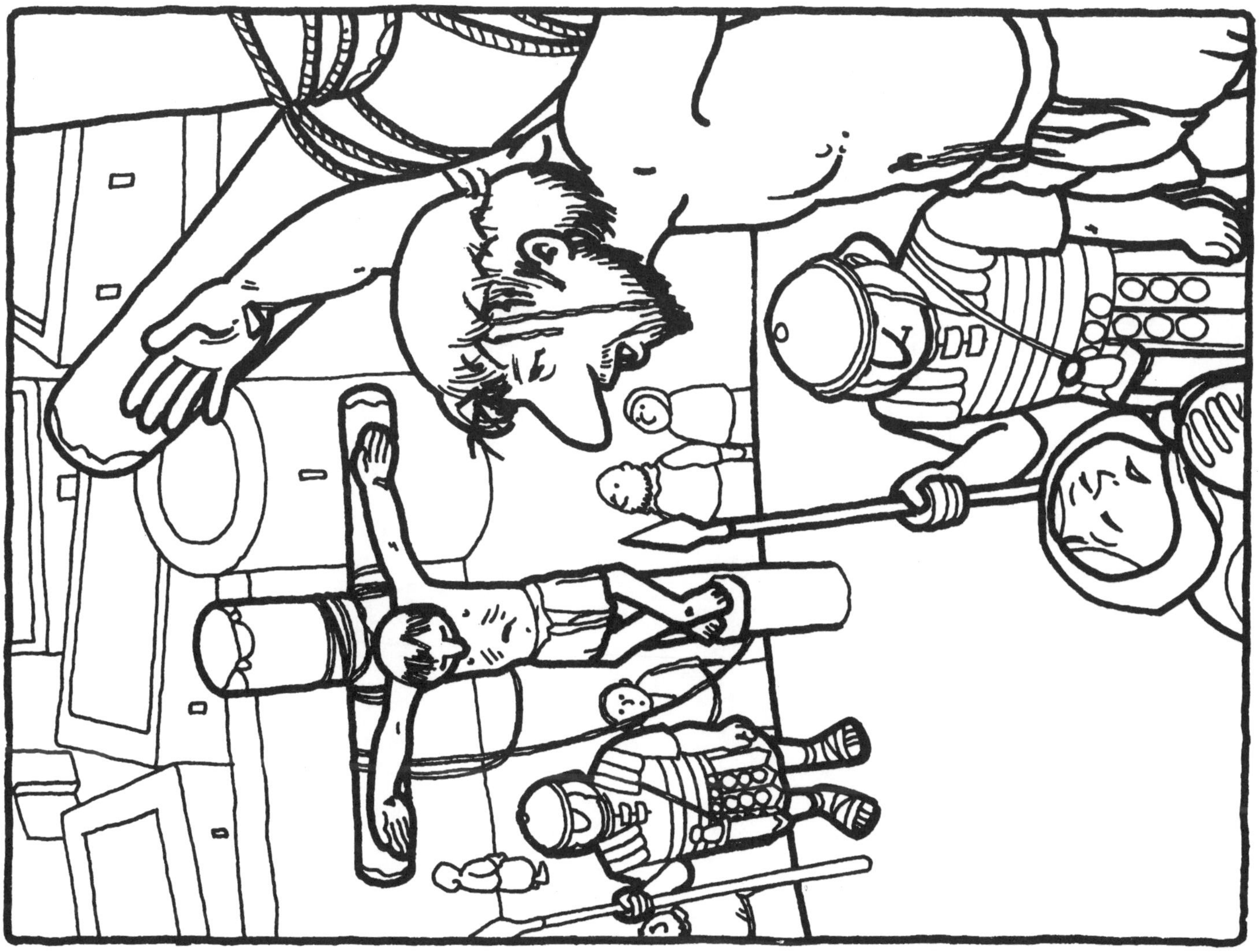

Jesus Is Risen

The full story is told in *Jesus Is Risen*,
ISBN 0 86209 366 X

Three days after Jesus had died, Mary Magdalene wanted to make sure everything was all right at the tomb. When she arrived, the big stone blocking the entrance had been rolled away and the tomb was empty!

Mary ran back to town and told Peter and John. She told them that someone had taken Jesus from the tomb. They quickly went to see for themselves.

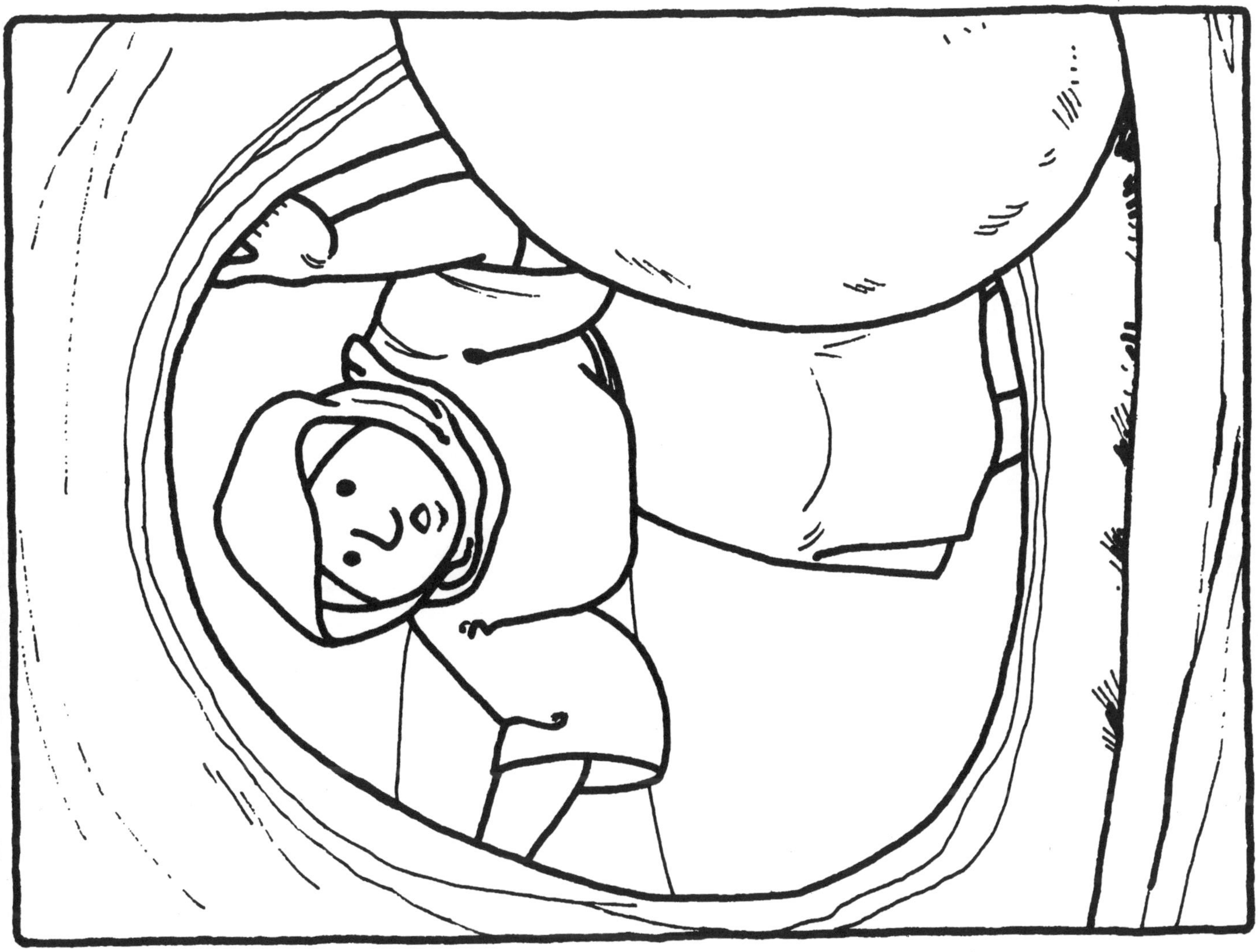

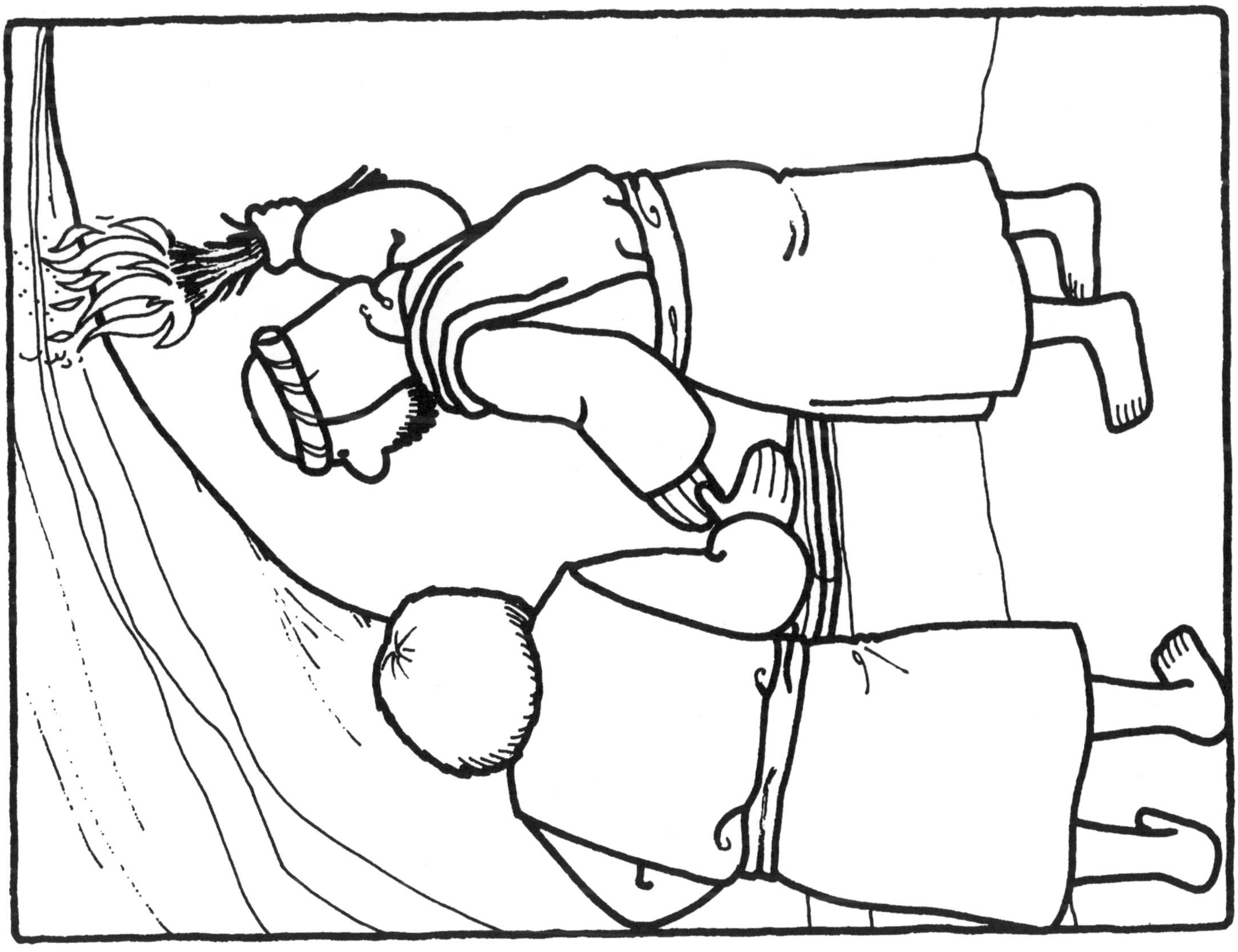

Mary sat outside the tomb, and suddenly saw two angels who asked her why she was crying. Then, somebody behind her said, 'Mary!' It was Jesus!

Mary ran and told all of Jesus' friends, but they didn't really believe her.

A few days later Jesus appeared to them all. Everyone jumped for joy!

Thomas wasn't there when Jesus had appeared and didn't believe what they told him. But a few days later, Jesus appeared again. Thomas touched him and knew that it was Jesus!

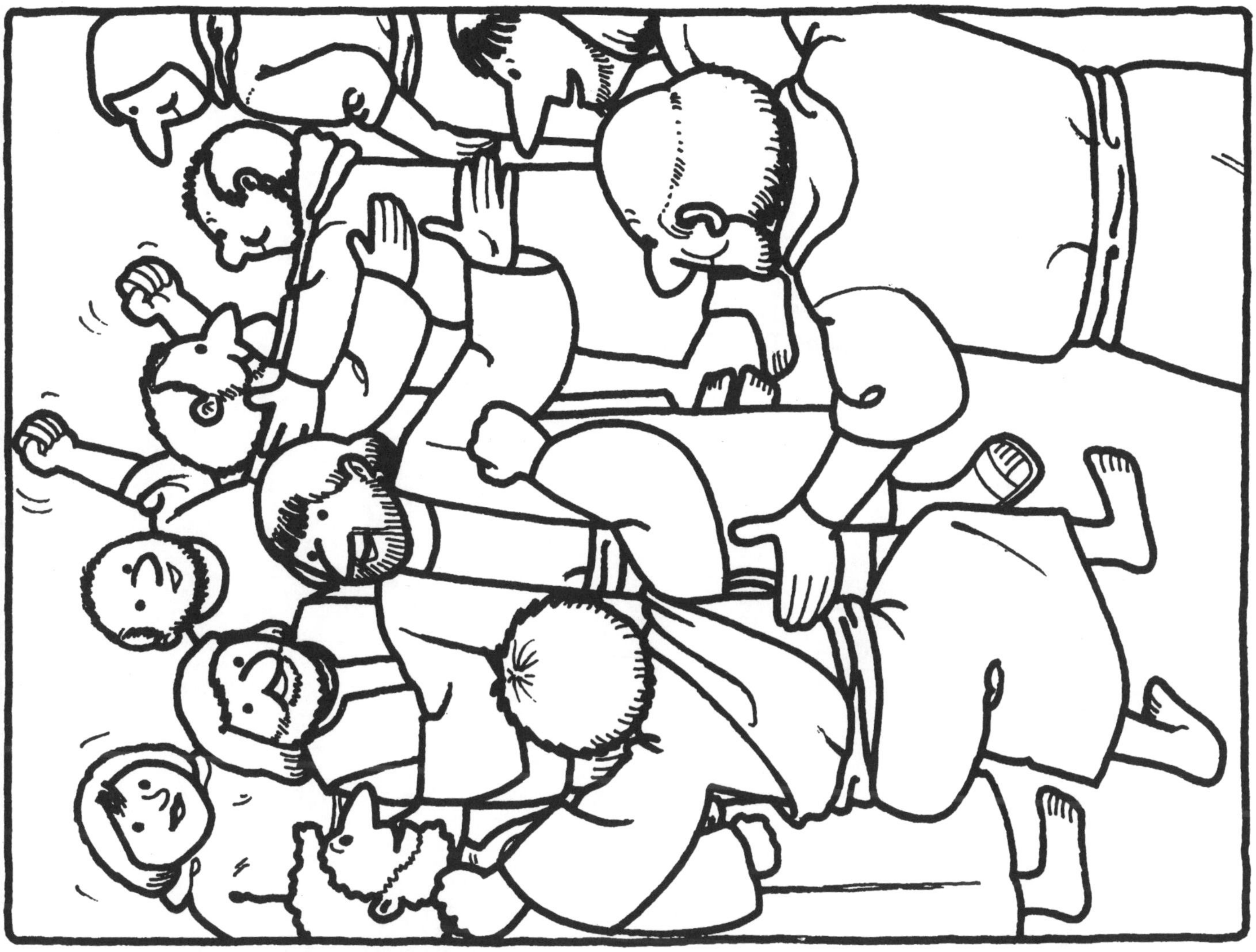

Peter in Prison

The full story is told in *Peter in Prison*,
ISBN 0 86209 523 9

King Herod hated Jesus' followers. His soldiers went round arresting them. They found Peter in the city and arrested him.

Peter's friends all prayed as hard as they could, asking God to look after Peter and to help him.

In the prison Peter was watched by four guards. He was sad and lonely, but he went on trusting God. At last, he nodded off to sleep.

An angel of God appeared and told Peter to follow him. The chains fell from Peter's wrists and ankles, and the soldiers didn't even notice!

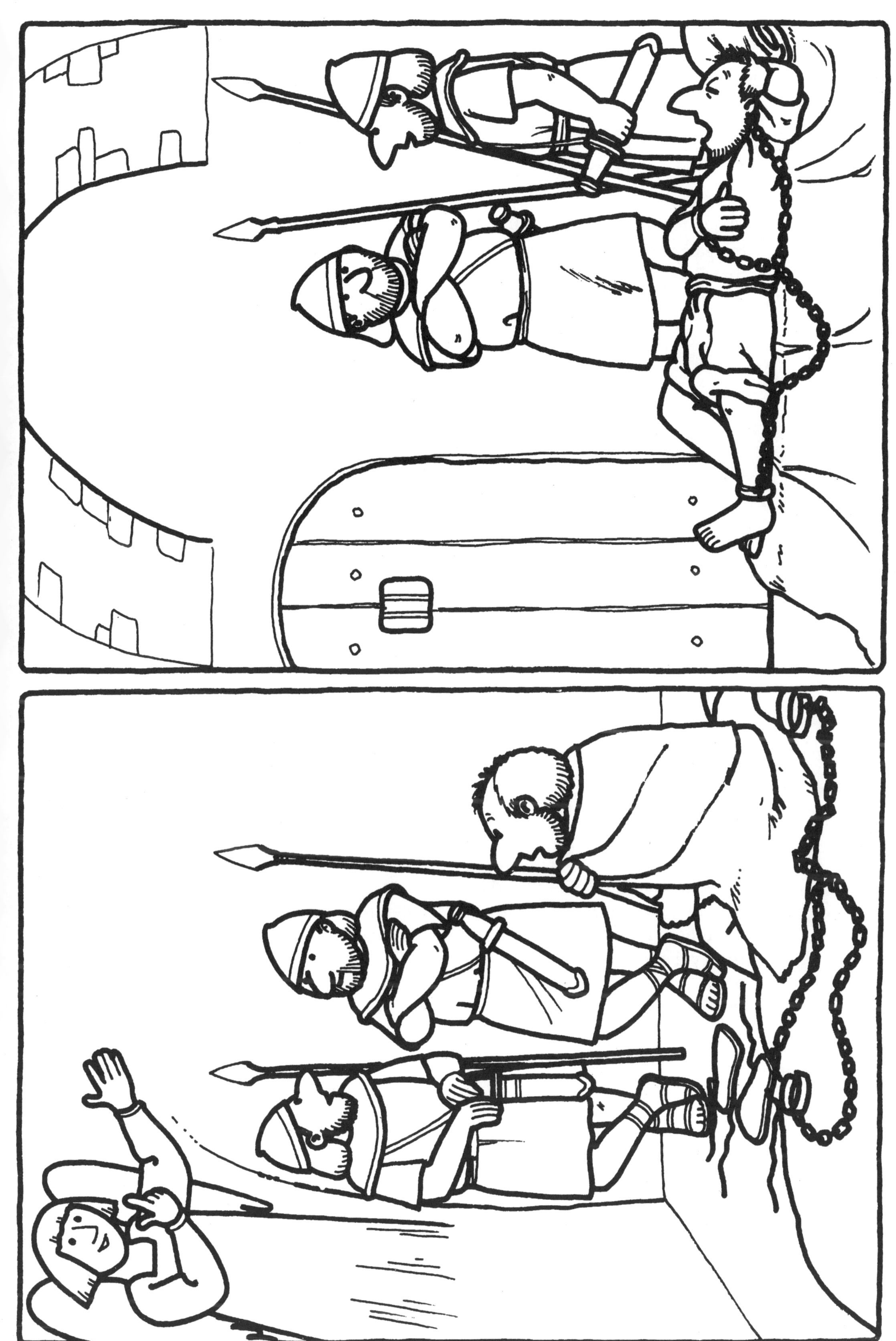

The angel led Peter past all the guards and through the gates to the city. The angel left Peter who realised that God had rescued him!

He ran straight to his friends' house. At first they couldn't believe it was really him! Peter then told them how the Lord had sent his angel to rescue him from prison.

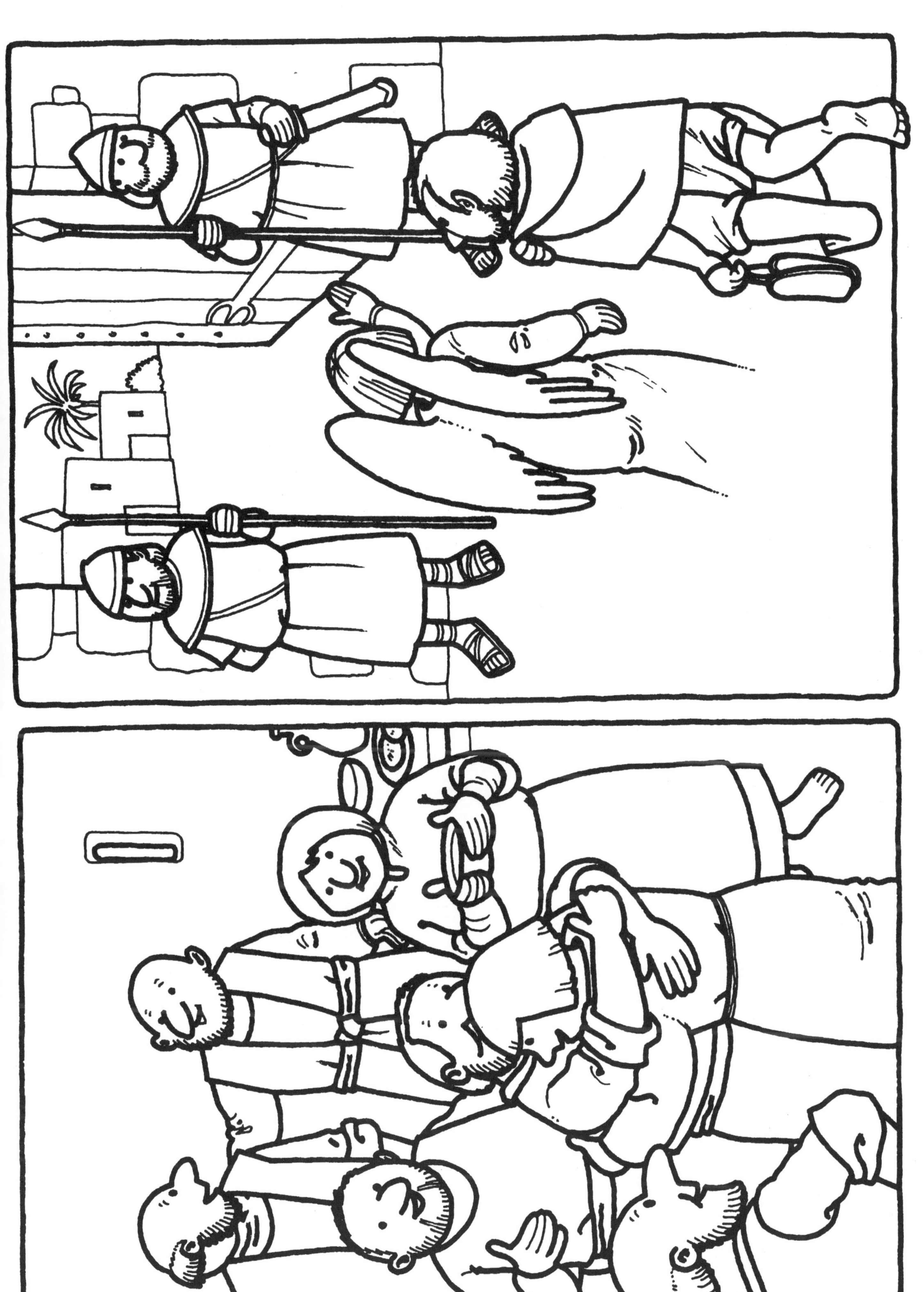